THE SECRET POWER OF GOD'S FAVOUR

Dr. Ephiel Mukamuri

THE SECRET POWER OF GOD'S FAVOUR

iUniverse books may be ordered through booksellers or by contacting:

iUniverse
1663 Liberty Drive
Bloomington, IN 47403
www.iuniverse.com
1-800-Authors (1-800-288-4677)

ISBN: 978-1-5320-9609-9 (sc)
ISBN: 978-1-5320-9610-5 (e)

Library of Congress Control Number: 2020905885

Print information available on the last page.

iUniverse rev. date: 03/26/2020

CONTENTS

ACKNOWLEDGMENTS

I give thanks to God the Father, Maker of heaven and earth, the Father of mercies. He has granted me exceeding abundant favours through the Lord Jesus Christ. **John 1:16, 17(nkjv)** "And of His fullness we have all received, and grace for grace. [17] For the law was given through Moses, *but* grace and truth came through Jesus Christ."

His Spirit of grace has and continues to administer JESUS' favours in my life, family and ministry.

I am grateful to God my Father for **Patrick Johnston** who led me in the prayer of receiving Christ in April of 1976. This was the time God's favour began to manifest in my life. I am also grateful to God for apostles, prophets, evangelists, pastors and teachers whom God has used to water my spiritual life.

I would also want to acknowledge my wife and co-labourer in the Gospel, **Tsungirayi Elna Mukamuri(nee Patsika)**, for loving me and being a blessing to me over the years. Thanks to our children, Charity, Theophilus, Shalom and Modercai; for just being there for me.

Finally, I thank God for the **Logos Rhema Ministries International Family** in different parts of the world. Together in Jesus' Name we are making a positive impact for God. May God's abundant favour increase, multiply and overwhelm you in Jesus' Name.

The message in this book is treasure for destiny! May God's favour always overwhelm you in Jesus' Name! Amen.

INTRODUCTION

God's favour is major secret in fulfilling kingdom purpose and vision. Every kingdom vision needs kingdom favour. This means favour with God and man. **Luke 2:52.** God`s favour is also commonly known or referred to as **DIVINE FAVOUR**.

In this book you shall come across a lot of references on GOD'S GRACE. The Greek word for grace is **CHARIS** which literally means **favour that cannot be earned. This is undeserved or unmerited favour.**

Divine favour is *neither a figment of human imagination nor a myth, IT IS REAL*. It is not natural, but supernatural. It is FROM GOD, BY GOD AND FOR GOD! God has availed it to ALL people through His Son Jesus Christ, but it is received by faith. The Apostle Paul wrote:

'By Whom (JESUS) also we have access by faith into this grace wherein we stand, ….'

Romans 5:2(kjv)

The Bible says *'And of His fullness have all we received, and grace for grace. For the law was given by Moses, but grace and truth came by Jesus Christ.'* **John 1:16-17(kjv)**

Under the New Testament, every child of God already has DIVINE FAVOUR based on **John 1:17.** This is because grace is UNMERITED/ UNDESERVED FAVOUR.

Salvation; which is man's greatest need, is FREELY available by God's favour to every man through the Lord Jesus Christ. What one has to do is to personally receive salvation by faith.

With Jesus Christ in your heart, let us travel the journey through this book together. You are headed for major breakthroughs. God's orchestrated favour will manifest in your life and great doors are going to open for you! Supernatural promotions are going to manifest for you because God is watching over His Word you are reading in this book to perform It.

"Then the LORD said to me, `You have seen well, for I am [actively] watching over My Word to fulfill it." **Jeremiah 1:12(Amp)**

Walking in God's favour does not mean a trouble or obstacle free life. Such things, the enemy will put in your way; but God's favour will override, frustrate, and humiliate all such satanic efforts as you stay in God's Word!

1

CHAPTER

THE GREAT ENTRANCE

*I*f you have not yet received Jesus in your heart; I am inviting you to open your heart for Him to come in. **Revelation 3:20.** This is how you receive God's free gift of SALVATION! Salvation through faith in Jesus Christ is THE HIGHEST and GREATEST MANIFESTATION of God's favour in a person's life. I call receiving salvation through Christ; THE GREAT ENTRANCE!

This is the only ETERNAL FAVOUR and it is the only ETERNAL MIRACLE! It also POSITIVELY influences the manifestation of ALL the other important favours we need as we live in this world. It is God's No1 priority for all people. It is coming out of Satan's kingdom into God's Kingdom! **Colossians1:13.** Jesus Christ said:

"But first *and* most importantly seek (aim at, strive after) His kingdom and His righteousness [His way of doing and being right—the attitude and character of God], and all these things will be given to you also." **Matthew 6:33(Amp)**

I am writing this important chapter on THE GREAT

ENTRANCE primarily for those who know that they are not yet saved or are not sure of their salvation through Jesus Christ. The message in the other chapters would be like putting cart before the horse unless salvation through Jesus Christ is a vital reality in your life. The Lord Jesus Christ said:

'For what shall it profit a man, if he shall gain the whole world and lose his own soul? Or what shall a man give in exchange for his soul?' Mark 8:36-37(kjv)

Receiving salvation is the entrance into divine favour. The Bible says by grace (God's unmerited favour) are you saved through faith. **Ephesians 2:8-9.** The gift of salvation is the greatest demonstration of God's favour towards mankind. In receiving salvation, one will be receiving God's FREE GIFT of **saving favour** through Jesus Christ.

In order to be saved one must do the following simple yet vital things:

1. Acknowledge that God loves you and has a good plan for your life. **Jeremiah 29:11.**
2. Acknowledge that because you are a descendant of Adam who sinned; you are a sinner by nature. **Psalms 51:5. Romans 5:12.**
3. Acknowledge that you have sinned **Isaiah 53:6, Romans 3:10, Romans 3:23**
4. Acknowledge that your sins have separated you from God and His good plan for your life**. Isaiah 59:1-2.**
5. Acknowledge that you cannot save yourself from your sins. **Isaiah 64:6, Jeremiah 13:23, Romans 7:24**
6. Acknowledge that you deserve to perish because of your sins. **Romans 6:23**
7. Acknowledge that God loved and loves you so much that He gave His Only Son Jesus Christ, who died a substitutionary death for you. Also acknowledge that Jesus Christ was buried and God raised Him from the

dead for you so that you will by faith in Him have eternal salvation. **John 3:16, Romans 4:25, Romans 5 :8**

8. Accept Jesus into your heart by faith, confessing Him as your personal Lord and Saviour. **Revelation 3:20, Ephesians 3:17, Romans 10:9-10.**

TO RECEIVE JESUS IN YOUR HEART, please pray the prayer below. The Bible says whosoever shall call upon the Name of the Lord shall be saved. **Romans 10:13.** Please pray whole heartedly, God is listening to you. He has been waiting for you to pray this prayer for a long time!

WHOLEHEARTEDLY PRAY:

"My loving God in Heaven, I acknowledge that I am a sinner and I cannot save myself. I know I deserve to go to hell because of my sins; but I thank you for giving me your Son Jesus, who died in my place so that I can be saved. I believe Jesus is your Son who died for me and rose from the dead.

I confess with my mouth that Jesus Christ is my Lord and I believe in my heart that You raised Him from the dead.

Please come into my heart Jesus, and be my Lord and my Saviour. I surrender my life into your loving care. Amen."

If you have prayed this prayer, according to God's Word you are now saved. You have embraced God's **FAVOUR AT THE HIGHEST LEVEL.** God and His angels are having a celebration in Heaven because of what you have just done! **Luke 15:1-10.** Your spirit man is now a new creation. **Titus 3:5, 2 Corinthians 5:17.** You are now God's child. **John 1:12. CONGRATULATIONS IN JESUS'NAME! AMEN!**

This is not the end, but the beginning of a new life... a new journey. In order to grow and become strong in this new life you need to:

1. Read your Bible…God's Word every day, **1 Peter 2:2** it is your spiritual FOOD!
2. Pray every day **Luke 18:1, 1Thesalonians 5:17**
3. Tell others that you have received salvation through Jesus Christ and INVITE them to receive Him too! **John 1:35-51, Mark 8:38.**
4. Become part of a Bible believing/practicing church, and connect with the pastors and positively get involved in the church activities. **Hebrews 10:25.**
5. I would also love to hear from you so I can pray for you and further encourage you in your new life in Christ.

My contact information is at the beginning and at the end of this book.

Please let us continue this great journey of studying on THE SECRET POWER OF GOD'S FAVOUR. God has more favour for you through Jesus Christ. It is grace on top of grace. **John 1:16.** It is manifold/multi-faceted favour. **1 Peter 4:10.**

2

CHAPTER

———⟨∞⟩———

DEFINITION OF GOD'S FAVOUR

*D*ivine favour is experiencing God's grace through Jesus Christ. In this grace, there is every good thing. **Psalms 84:11**. There is **every spiritual blessing. Ephesians 1:3**. There is **redemption from every curse**; and **empowerment to prosper through Abraham's blessing. Galatians 3:13-14.** There is **exceeding abundantly, far above all we can ask or even imagine. Ephesians 3:20.**

In simple biblical terms, Divine Favour is:

1. **Experiencing God's grace through Jesus Christ in salvation. John 1:16-17, Titus 2:11, Ephesians 2:8, Titus 3:5.**
2. **Being shown astonishing, unexpected, mind boggling extravagant kindness through God's influence. The Bible has the testimonies of;**

   *Moses: shown kindness by Pharaoh's daughter and her family **Exodus 2:5-10**
   * **Mephibosheth: 2 Samuel 9:1-13.** Shown kindness by David, which took him from the guerrilla outpost in Lo Debar,

to inherit the royal estate of King Saul and also eat in the palace at the king's table with the princes PERMANENTLY.

*Esther: Esther 2:8-9. Esther found favour in the sight of Hegai the keeper of the women in the king's palace. She was allocated the best quarters in the king's palace together with her women.

3. **It means experiencing supernatural experiences.**

*Esther: Esther 2:15-18. King Ahasuerus married and lived with Esther without knowing her family and nationality. More than once he offered her half of his kingdom without knowing her nationality.

*Joseph: Genesis 41:37-43, Acts 7:10. Joseph, a slave, convict and foreigner was promoted to become governor of Egypt to the delight of Pharaoh and all his leadership.

4. **Supernatural goodwill**

*Jonathan: 1 Samuel 14:45-46, Saul's soldiers refused to carry out Saul's command to kill Jonathan.

*Mordecai: Esther 10:1-3. Mordecai, a foreigner and an exile/captive, was promoted to become second in the kingdom of Persia.

5. **Supernatural promotions:** Joseph, Mordecai and Daniel. All these three were supernaturally promoted through divine favour. They became second to the kings in the countries they lived after God promoted them.
6. **Favour also manifests in the form of Supernatural protection and provision.**

*David: 1 Samuel 27:1- When David was running away from Saul, he fled to the land of the Philistines. God gave David favour in the sight of Achish king of Gath and he stayed there permanently until the death of Saul. David was given refuge and a city permanently by the Philistines. **1 Samuel 27:5-6**

7. **The favour of God can cause you to be supernaturally used by God.**

* **Mary: Luke 1:28.** Mary became the mother of our Lord Jesus being historically singled out by God for unique assignments.

DIVINE FAVOUR WILL SINGLE YOU OUT TO SUCCESSFULLY CARRY OUT UNIQUE ASSIGNMENTS THAT YOU PERSONALLY FEEL YOU ARE NOT QUALIFIED TO CARRY OUT. IT BRINGS HONOURABLE MANDATES FROM GOD OF WHICH ONE MIGHT FEEL HE OR SHE DOES NOT DESERVE.

3

—∞∞∞—

HOW TO WALK AND INCREASE IN DIVINE FAVOUR

*R*emember favour cannot be earned and yet there are things a child of God can do to provoke an increase of it in one's life. Always take note that favour far outweighs anything any child of God can do. If you are God's child you already have the favour of God.

1. Acknowledge the reality of divine favour. It would be futile for you to trust God for and pursue a UTOPIA, your heart must believe in the reality of divine favour. It is not a myth, it is real. Trust the Holy Spirit, who guides us into all the truth to reveal the reality and the vitality of divine favour to your spirit man. **John 14:26, John 16:13**

2. Acknowledge that because you have received Jesus Christ and you are born again, you have God's favour in your life and you are God's favourite. **John 1:16-17; Ephesians 2:8-9, Titus 3:5.**

3. Acknowledge that Jesus Christ is your righteousness, **1 Corinthians 1:30** and you are the righteousness of

God through Christ. **2 Corinthians 5:21.** God has given you the gift of righteousness **Romans 5:17,** that you are justified by faith **Romans 5:1,** YOU ARE THUS A RIGHTEOUS MAN. Since you are righteous you can BOLDLY CLAIM **Psalms 5:12** which says that God surrounds the righteous with favour as with a shield! Do so by FAITH.

4. Acknowledge that Christ is your wisdom **1 Cor. 1:30, Col 2:3, Proverbs 8:35** because favour follows the wise.

5. Walk humbly with God because God gives grace to the humble **James 4:6, 1 Peter 5:5-6.** Though you have favour, you need more favour.

6. Believe God for and strive for excellence because it promotes your finding favour. Get rid of all mediocrity and compromise in your work and service for God. **Daniel 6:1-3.** By God's help it is possible. **Philippians 2:13.**

7. Be a man or a woman of integrity. Desire and trust God for faithfulness. Study it in God's Word. Believe God to manifest His faithfulness through you. This promotes favour in a big way. **Matthew 25:21-23, Luke 12:42-44**

8. Desire more of God's favour and ask God for it in faith **Hebrews 4:16; Matthew 21:22. 1 John 5:14**

9. Sow favour into the lives of others. Mordecai did all he could for the promotion of Esther to become queen. He got his harvest. **Esther2:5-8; 6:10-11, 8:1-2, 10:1-3**

10. Celebrate divine favour in the lives of others. Never ever stand in the way of God's favour for someone. It is dangerous (a) Saul fought God's favour in David's life and it did not go well with him (b) Aaron celebrated God's favour in his brother(Moses') life and God increased him. He started to walk in God's favour too and increased!

11. Associate with people who are walking in God's favour and learn the wisdom to walk in God's favour too, also get some impartation. **Romans 1:11-12**

12. Be friendly, and be a good person. Trust God to be a blessing to others. Dorcas was such a one and when she died the saints at Joppa sent for Peter and she was raised from the dead. **Acts 9:36-40**, also see **Proverbs 12:2**

4

CHAPTER

———— ∞∞∞ ————

DIVINE APPOINTMENTS FOR DIVINE FAVOUR.

A divine appointment is a meeting of two or more individuals or parties orchestrated by God in order to facilitate the fulfilment of their God given destiny. No man can arrange a divine appointment. Otherwise it would no longer be divine but just a natural human appointment.

Divine appointments are also God's instruments of acceleration. Sometimes the parties involved in a divine appointment are fully unaware that it is a divine appointment. Many a time they realise it much later.

God can use human instrumentation, but no man can either make or create a divine appointment. In most cases they come as surprise unplanned meetings. A child of God can 'stumble' into divine appointments unaware.

Sometimes divine appointments are preceded by painful failures and disappointments. This is because we many a time need to disengage from certain relationships, connections and expectations in order to connect to relationships of destiny. The divine appointments are platforms God has set up for ushering us into divine favour. They precede the coming attraction called manifestation of divine favour. The Lord has the scripts for all these episodes.

5

CHAPTER

※

EXAMPLES OF PEOPLE WHO EXPERIENCED DIVINE FAVOUR

1. NOAH

'And God saw that the wickedness of man was great in the earth, and that the imagination of the thoughts of his heart was only evil continually. And it repented the Lord that He had made man on the earth and that it grieved Him at His heart. And the LORD said, "1 will destroy man whom 1 have created from the face of the earth: both man and the beast, and the creeping thing, the fowls of the air, for it repented me that 1 have made them. **"BUT NOAH FOUND GRACE IN THE EYES OF THE LORD" Genesis 6:7-8(kjv)**

2. JACOB

"For the children being not yet born, neither having done any good or evil, that the purpose of God according to election, might stand, not of works but of Him that calleth. It was said unto her, the elder shall serve the younger. As it is written, Jacob have 1 loved, but Esau have 1 hated." **Romans 9:11-13(kjv)**

"What shall we say then? Is there unrighteousness with God? God forbid. For He saith to Moses, 1 will have mercy on whom 1 will have mercy and compassion on whom 1 will have compassion. So then it is not of him that willeth, nor of him that runneth, but of God that sheweth mercy." **Romans 9:14-16(kjv)**

3. **JOSEPH**

'Now Israel loved Joseph more than all his children, because he was the son of his old age: and he made him a coat of many colours.' **Genesis 37:3(kjv)**

'And his master saw that the LORD was with him, and that the LORD made all that he did to prosper in his hand. And Joseph found grace in his sight, and he served him: and he made him overseer over his house, and all that he had he put into his hand.' **Genesis 39: 3-4(kjv)**

'But the LORD was with Joseph, and shewed him mercy, and gave him favour in the sight of the keeper of the prison. And the keeper of the prison committed to Joseph's hand all the prisoners that [were] in the prison; and whatsoever they did there, he was the doer [of it]'. **Genesis 39:21-22(kjv)**

'And the thing was good in the eyes of Pharaoh, and in the eyes of all his servants. And Pharaoh said unto his servants, "Can we find [such a one] as this [is], a man in whom the Spirit of God [is]?" And Pharaoh said unto Joseph, "Forasmuch as God hath shewed thee all this, [there is] none so discreet and wise as thou [art]: Thou shalt be over my house, and according unto thy word shall all my people be ruled: only in the throne will I be greater than thou". And Pharaoh said unto Joseph ", See, I have set thee over all the land of Egypt." And Pharaoh took off his ring from his hand, and put it upon Joseph's hand, and arrayed him in vestures of fine linen, and put a gold chain about his neck; And he made him to ride in the second chariot which he had; and they cried before him, "Bow the knee": and he made him [ruler] over all the land of Egypt. And Pharaoh said unto Joseph, "I [am] Pharaoh, and without thee shall no man lift up his hand or foot in all the land of Egypt." And Pharaoh called Joseph's name Zaphnathpaaneah; and he gave him to wife Asenath the daughter of Potipherah priest of On. And Joseph went out over [all] the land of Egypt. **Genesis 41: 37-45(kjv)**

'And delivered him out of all his afflictions, and gave him favour and wisdom in the sight of Pharaoh king of Egypt; and he made him governor over Egypt and all his house.' **Acts 7:10(kjv)**

4. MOSES

Pharaoh had given a charge that all new born Hebrew boys were supposed to be thrown into the river Nile but Moses found favour:

Before his parents: "And the woman conceived, and bare a son: and when she saw him that he [was a] goodly [child], she hid him three months. And when she could not longer hide him, she took for him an ark of bulrushes, and daubed it with slime and with pitch, and put the child therein; and she laid [it] in the flags by the river's brink.' **Exodus 2:2-3(kjv)**

Before Pharaoh's daughter: 'And the daughter of Pharaoh came down to wash [herself] at the river; and her maidens walked along by the river's side; and when she saw the ark among the flags, she sent her maid to fetch it. And when she had opened [it], she saw the child: and, behold, the babe wept. And she had compassion on him, and said, "This [is one] of the Hebrews' children". Then said his sister to Pharaoh's daughter, "Shall I go and call to thee a nurse of the Hebrew women, that she may nurse the child for thee?" And Pharaoh's daughter said to her, "Go." And the maid went and called the child's mother. And Pharaoh's daughter said unto her, "Take this child away, and nurse it for me, and I will give [thee] thy wages". And the woman took the child, and nursed it. And the child grew, and she brought him unto Pharaoh's daughter, and he became her son. And she called his name Moses: and she said, "Because I drew him out of the water." **Exodus 2:5-10(kjv)**

Before Pharaoh for 40 years

Definitely Pharaoh knew about his daughter's 'Hebrew son' and yet in spite of his charge to get Hebrew baby boys killed, he spared Moses. He raised the Deliverer of God's people, gave him what could be called 'Harvard or Yale' standard of education at the Egyptian treasury's expense. He housed, clothed, fed, and protected him as though he was of the Egyptian Royal family. Mind you, Egypt was a super power then. It was the leader in agriculture, industry, commerce and civilization. Moses had first class- royal class experiences by Divine favour.

5. THE CHILDREN OF ISRAEL BEFORE THE EGYPTIANS

"And He said to Abram, know of a surety that thy seed shall be a stranger in a land that is not theirs, and shall serve them and they shall afflict them for four hundred years, and also that nation, whom they shall serve, will l judge and afterwards shall they come out with great substance" **Genesis 15:13-14(kjv)**

"And l will give this people favour in the sight of the Egyptians: and it shall come to pass, that, when ye go, ye shall not go empty

"But every woman shall borrow of their neighbour and her that sojourneth in her house, jewels of silver and jewels of gold and raiment and you shall put them upon your sons, and upon your daughters; AND YE SHALL SPOIL THE EGYPTIANS" **Exodus 3:21-22(kjv)**

"Speak now in the ears of the people, and let every man borrow of his neighbour and every woman of her neighbour, jewels of silver and jewels of gold." And the LORD gave the people favour in the sight of the Egyptians. Moreover, the man Moses was very great in the land of Egypt, in the sight of Pharaoh's servants, and in the sight of the people' **Exodus 11:2-3(kjv)**

'And the children of Israel did according to the word of Moses, and they borrowed of the Egyptians, jewels of silver and jewels of gold, and raiment. And the LORD gave the people favour in the sight of the Egyptians, so that they lent unto them such things as they required, and they spoiled the Egyptians.' **Exodus 12:35-36(kjv)**

'He brought them forth also with silver and gold and there was not one feeble person among their tribes. Egypt was glad when they departed, for the fear of them fell upon them.' **Psalm 105:37-38(kjv)**

6. SAMUEL

'And the child grew on, and was in favour both with the LORD and also with men' **I Samuel 2:26(kjv)**

'And Samuel grew, and the LORD was with him and did let none of His words fall to the ground. And all Israel from Dan even Beersheba knew that Samuel was established to be a prophet of the LORD And the LORD appeared again in Shiloh: for the LORD revealed Himself to Samuel in Shiloh by the Word of the Lord'. **I Samuel 3:19-21(kjv)**

7. DAVID

God gave David favour with Israel's men of war and all Israel. The Bible says;

"All these men of war, that could keep rank, came with a perfect heart to Hebron, to make David king over all Israel: and all the rest also of Israel were of one heart to make David king. And there they were with David three days, eating and drinking: for their brethren had prepared for them." **1 Chronicles 12:38-39(kjv)**

8. NEHEMIAH

Nehemiah prayed to God for favour before the king. "Oh Lord, 1 beseech thee, let now Thine ear be attentive to the prayer of Your servant and to the prayer of Thy servants, who desire to fear Thy Name and prosper them I pray thee. Favour thy servant this day and GRANT HIM MERCY in the sight of this man. For I was the king's cupbearer." **Nehemiah 1:11(kjv)**

And Nehemiah spoke to the king:

"And I said unto the king, if it pleases the king, and if thy servant has found FAVOUR in thy sight, that thou wouldest send me unto Judah unto the city of my fathers' sepulchres, that I may build it:" **Nehemiah 2:5(kjv)**

Nehemiah received favour:

"……. And the king GRANTED ME, ACCORDING to the GOOD HAND of my GOD upon me." **Nehemiah 2:8b(kjv)**

9. ESTHER

"And the maiden pleased him and she obtained kindness of him and speedily gave her things for purification, with such things as belonged to her and seven maidens, which were meet to be given her out of the king's house and he preferred her and unto her maidens unto the best place of the house of the women" **Esther 2:9(kjv)**

'Now the turn of Esther, the daughter of Abihail the uncle of Mordecai, who had taken her for his daughter, was come to go in unto the king, she required nothing but what Hegai the king's chamberlain, the keeper of the women, appointed. And Esther obtained favour in the sight of all them that looked upon her. So Esther was taken unto king Ahasuerus into his house royal in the tenth month which is the month Tebeth, in the seventh year of his reign. And the king loved Esther above all women, and she obtained grace and favour in his sight more than all the virgins, so that he set the royal crown upon her head and made her queen instead of Vashti. Then the king made a great feast unto all his princes and his servants, even Esther's feast and he made a release to the provinces and gave gifts according to the state of the king:' **Esther 2:15-18(kjv)**

'And it was so, when the king saw Esther the queen standing in the court that she obtained favour in his sight and the king held out to Esther the golden sceptre. Then said the king unto her, "What wilt thou, Queen Esther? And what is thy request? It shall be given thee to half of the kingdom" And Esther answered, "If it seems good unto the king, let the king and Haman come this day unto the banquet that I have prepared for him." Then the king said, "Cause Haman to make haste that he may do as Esther hath said." So the King and Haman came to the Banquet that Esther had prepared.' **Esther 5:2-5(kjv)**

'And the king said unto Esther at the banquet of wine, "What is thy petition? And it shall be granted thee: and what is thy request even unto half the kingdom it shall be performed." Then answered Esther, and said "My Petition and my request is: If I have found favour in the sight of the king, and if it please the king to grant my petition, and to perform my request, let the king and Haman come to the banquet that I shall prepare for them, and I will do tomorrow as the king has said:" **Esther 5:6-8(kjv)**

'And the king said again unto Esther on the second day at the banquet of wine. "What is thy petition, Queen Esther? And it shall be granted thee and what is thy request? and it shall be performed even unto half the kingdom" Then Esther the queen answered and said, "If I have found favour in thy sight, O king and if it pleases the king, let my life be given me at my petition and my people at my request. For, we are sold; I and my people, to be destroyed, to be slain and to perish. But if we had been sold for bondmen and bondwomen, I had held my tongue, although the enemy could not countervail the king's damage." Then the king Ahasuesus answered and said unto Esther, the queen, "Who is he and where is he, that durst presume in his heart to do so?" And Esther said, "The adversary and enemy is this wicked Haman". Then Haman was afraid before the king and the queen and the king arising from the banquet of wine in his wrath went into the palace garden, and Haman stood up to make request for his life to Esther the queen, for he saw that there was evil determined against him by the king. Then the king returned out of the palace garden into the place of the banquet of wine, and Haman was fallen upon the bed whereon Esther was. Then said the king, "Will he force the queen also before me in the house?" As the word went out of the king's mouth, they covered Haman's face and Harbonah, one of the chamberlains said before the king, "Behold also, the gallows fifty cubits high which Haman had made for Mordecai, who had spoken good for the king standeth in the house of Haman." Then, the King said, "Hang him thereon."

So they hanged Haman on the gallows that he had prepared for Mordecai. Then was the king's wrath pacified.' **Esther 7:2-10(kjv)**

10. **MORDECAI**

"On that night could not the king sleep, and he commanded to bring the book of records of the chronicles; and they were read before the king.

And it was found written, that Mordecai had told of Bigthana and Teresh, two of the king's chamberlains, the keepers of the door, who sought to lay hand on the king Ahasuerus.

And the king said, what honour and dignity hath been done to Mordecai for this? Then said the king's servants that ministered unto him, there is nothing done for him.

And the king said, who is in the court? Now Haman was come into the outward court of the king's house, to speak unto the king to hang Mordecai on the gallows that he had prepared for him.

And the king's servants said unto him, Behold, Haman standeth in the court. And the king said, let him come in.

So Haman came in. And the king said unto him, what shall be done unto the man whom the king delighteth to honour? Now Haman thought in his heart, to whom would the king delight to do honour more than to myself?

And Haman answered the king, For the man whom the king delighteth to honour,

Let the royal apparel be brought which the king useth to

wear, and the horse that the king rideth upon, and the crown royal which is set upon his head:

And let this apparel and horse be delivered to the hand of one of the king's most noble princes, that they may array the man withal whom the king delighteth to honour, and bring him on horseback through the street of the city, and proclaim before him, thus shall it be done to the man whom the king delighteth to honour.

Then the king said to Haman, make haste, and take the apparel and the horse, as thou hast said, and do even so to Mordecai the Jew, that sitteth at the king's gate: let nothing fail of all that thou hast spoken.

Then took Haman the apparel and the horse, and arrayed Mordecai, and brought him on horseback through the street of the city, and proclaimed before him, thus shall it be done unto the man whom the king delighteth to honour.

And Mordecai came again to the king's gate. But Haman hasted to his house mourning, and having his head covered.

And Haman told Zeresh his wife and all his friends every thing that had befallen him. Then said his wise men and Zeresh his wife unto him, If Mordecai be of the seed of the Jews, before whom thou hast begun to fall, thou shalt not prevail against him, but shalt surely fall before him." **Esther 6:1-13(kjv)**

"And Harbonah, one of the chamberlains, said before the king, behold also, the gallows fifty cubits high, which Haman had made for Mordecai, who had spoken good for the king, standeth in the house of Haman. Then the king said, Hang him thereon.

So they hanged Haman on the gallows that he had prepared for Mordecai. Then was the king's wrath pacified." **Esther 7:9-10(kjv)**

"And all the rulers of the provinces, and the lieutenants, and the deputies, and officers of the king, helped the Jews; because the fear of Mordecai fell upon them.

For Mordecai was great in the king's house, and his fame

went out throughout all the provinces: for this man Mordecai waxed greater and greater.

Thus the Jews smote all their enemies with the stroke of the sword, and slaughter, and destruction, and did what they would unto those that hated them. And in Shushan the palace the Jews slew and destroyed five hundred men. And Parshandatha, and Dalphon, and Aspatha, And Poratha, and Adalia, and Aridatha, And Parmashta, and Arisai, and Aridai, and Vajezatha, the ten sons of Haman the son of Hammedatha, the enemy of the Jews, slew they; but on the spoil laid they not their hand. On that day the number of those that were slain in Shushan the palace was brought before the king." **Esther 9:3-11(kjv)**

"And all the acts of his power and of his might, and the declaration of the greatness of Mordecai, whereunto the king advanced him, are they not written in the book of the chronicles of the kings of Media and Persia?

For Mordecai the Jew was next unto king Ahasuerus, and great among the Jews, and accepted of the multitude of his brethren, seeking the wealth of his people, and speaking peace to all his seed." **Esther 10:2-3(kjv)**

11. DANIEL

Now God had brought Daniel into favour and tender love with the prince of the eunuchs: **Daniel 1:9(kjv)**

'It pleased Daniel to set over the kingdom a hundred and twenty princes, which should be over the whole kingdom. And over these three presidents of whom Daniel was first: that the princes might give accounts unto them, and the king should have no damage. Then this Daniel was preferred above the presidents and princes, because an excellent spirit was in him, and the king thought to set him over the whole realm:' **Daniel 6:1-3(kjv)**

12. CYRUS KING OF PERSIA

'Thus saith the LORD to His anointed, to Cyrus, whose right hand I have holden to subdue nations before him and I will loose the loins of kings, to open before him the two leaved gates; and the gates shall not be shut.

'I will go before thee, and make the crooked places straight. I will break in pieces the gates of brass and cut asunder the bars of iron. And I will give thee the treasures of darkness and hidden riches of secret places.' **Isaiah 45:1-3(kjv)**

'That thou mayest know that I, the LORD, which call thee by name, and the God of Israel. For Jacob my servant's sake and Israel mine elect, I have even called thee by name. I have summoned thee, though thou has not know me. I am the LORD and there is no god beside me. I girded thee, though thou hast not known me.' **Isaiah 45:3b-5(kjv)**

Cyrus was given favour by God to become a rich and powerful emperor in order to serve God's purpose of releasing and empowering Jews to go back to Jerusalem and build God's house. He did just that: **Ezra 1:1-11.** What Jeremiah prophesied in **Jeremiah 29:10-14** was fulfilled. If a heathen king could serve God's purpose so willingly, how much more a born again child of God?

13. **THE JEWS OF THE DAYS OF KING CYRUS**

These are the Jews who were in the Persian Empire during the days of King Cyrus. Some of them went back to Jerusalem after Cyrus made a favourable decree. Cyrus' decree was as follows:

"Thus saith Cyrus king of Persia, The LORD God of heaven hath given me all the kingdoms of the earth; and he hath charged me to build him a house at Jerusalem, which is in Judah.

Who is there among you of all his people? his God be with him, and let him go up to Jerusalem, which is in Judah, and build the house of the LORD God of Israel, (he is the God,) which is in Jerusalem.

And whosoever remaineth in any place where he sojourneth, let the men of his place help him with silver, and with gold, and with goods, and with beasts, beside the freewill offering for the house of God that is in Jerusalem." **Ezra 1:2-4(kjv)**

Cyrus, the king of Persia also availed vast quantities of articles for the Jews who desired to return to Jerusalem to carry them back. The Bible says;

"Also Cyrus the king brought forth the vessels of the house of the LORD, which Nebuchadnezzar had brought forth out of Jerusalem, and had put them in the house of his gods;

Even those did Cyrus king of Persia bring forth by the hand of Mithredath the treasurer, and numbered them unto Sheshbazzar, the prince of Judah.

And this is the number of them: thirty chargers of gold, a thousand chargers of silver, nine and twenty knives,

Thirty basons/basins of gold, silver basons/basins of a second sort four hundred and ten, and other vessels a thousand.

All the vessels of gold and of silver were five thousand and four hundred. All these did Sheshbazzar bring up with them of the captivity that were brought up from Babylon unto Jerusalem." **Ezra 1:7-11(kjv)**

Construction began successfully, but the enemies of Jerusalem caused the work to cease after they slandered Jerusalem.

In **Ezra 4:1-24,** we read that the work eventually ceased by king Darius' instruction because of the slander of the enemies of Jerusalem. But a request was sent to the king for a search to be made amongst the records in the treasure house of the king's house. The Bible thus says:

"Now therefore, if it seems good to the king, let there be search made in the king's treasure house, which is there at Babylon, whether it be so, that a decree was made of Cyrus the king to build this house of God at Jerusalem, and let the king send his pleasure to us concerning this matter." **Ezra 5:17(kjv)**

After the search was done; the decree made by King Cyrus was found as recorded in Ezra 6: 1-7. In all this we see the manifestation of divine favour because in the light of the discovery of this decree king Darius issued a decree in favour of the continuation of the building of the temple in Jerusalem. The decree said thus:

"Moreover I make a decree what ye shall do to the elders of these Jews for the building of this house of God: that of the king's goods, even of the tribute beyond the river, forthwith expenses be given unto these men, that they be not hindered.

And that which they have need of, both young bullocks, and rams, and lambs, for the burnt offerings of the God of heaven, wheat, salt, wine, and oil, according to the appointment of the priests which are at Jerusalem, let it be given them day by day without fail:

That they may offer sacrifices of sweet savours unto the God of heaven, and pray for the life of the king, and of his sons.

Also I have made a decree, that whosoever shall alter this word, let timber be pulled down from his house, and being set up, let him be hanged thereon; and let his house be made a dunghill for this.

And the God that hath caused His Name to dwell there destroy all kings and people, that shall put to their hand to alter and to destroy this house of God which is at Jerusalem. I Darius have made a decree; let it be done with speed." **Ezra 6: 8-12(kjv)**

Because of favour from God through king Darius everything the king decreed was done speedily and the temple was built and finished. The priests did their ministry and the Jews in Jerusalem celebrated the Passover and Feast of Unleavened Bread.

14. **EZRA BEFORE KING ARTAXERXES**

Ezra and the Jews experienced favour in the days of king Artaxerxes. King Artaxerxes made a decree similar to the decrees previously made by King Cyrus and king Darius.

"Now after these things, in the reign of Artaxerxes king of Persia, Ezra the son of Seraiah, the son of Azariah, the son of Hilkiah,

The son of Shallum, the son of Zadok, the son of Ahitub,

The son of Amariah, the son of Azariah, the son of Meraioth,

The son of Zerahiah, the son of Uzzi, the son of Bukki,

The son of Abishua, the son of Phinehas, the son of Eleazar, the son of Aaron the chief priest:

This Ezra went up from Babylon; and he was a ready scribe in the law of Moses, which the LORD God of Israel had given: and the king granted him all his request, according to the hand of the LORD his God upon him.

And there went up some of the children of Israel, and of the priests, and the Levites, and the singers, and the porters, and the Nethinims, unto Jerusalem, in the seventh year of Artaxerxes the king.

And he came to Jerusalem in the fifth month, which was in the seventh year of the king.

For upon the first day of the first month began he to go up from Babylon, and on the first day of the fifth month came he to Jerusalem, according to the good hand of his God upon him.

For Ezra had prepared his heart to seek the law of the LORD, and to do it, and to teach in Israel statutes and judgments.

Now this is the copy of the letter that the king Artaxerxes gave unto Ezra the priest, the scribe, even a scribe of the words of the commandments of the LORD, and of His statutes to Israel.

Artaxerxes, king of kings, unto Ezra the priest, a scribe of the law of the God of heaven, perfect peace, and at such a time.

I make a decree, that all they of the people of Israel, and of his priests and Levites, in my realm, which are minded of their own freewill to go up to Jerusalem, go with thee.

Forasmuch as thou art sent of the king, and of his seven counsellors, to enquire concerning Judah and Jerusalem, according to the law of thy God which is in thine hand;

And to carry the silver and gold, which the king and his counsellors have freely offered unto the God of Israel, whose habitation is in Jerusalem,

And all the silver and gold that thou canst find in all the province of Babylon, with the freewill offering of the people, and of the priests, offering willingly for the house of their God which is in Jerusalem:

That thou mayest buy speedily with this money bullocks, rams, lambs, with their meat offerings and their drink offerings, and offer them upon the altar of the house of your God which is in Jerusalem.

And whatsoever shall seem good to thee, and to thy brethren, to do with the rest of the silver and the gold, that do after the will of your God.

The vessels also that are given thee for the service of the house of thy God, those deliver thou before the God of Jerusalem.

And whatsoever more shall be needful for the house of thy God, which thou shalt have occasion to bestow, bestow it out of the king's treasure house.

And I, even I Artaxerxes the king, do make a decree to all the treasurers which are beyond the river, that whatsoever Ezra the priest, the scribe of the law of the God of heaven, shall require of you, it be done speedily,

Unto a hundred talents of silver, and to a hundred measures of wheat, and to a hundred baths of wine, and to a hundred baths of oil, and salt without prescribing how much.

Whatsoever is commanded by the God of heaven, let it be diligently done for the house of the God of heaven: for why should there be wrath against the realm of the king and his sons?

Also we certify you, that touching any of the priests and Levites, singers, porters, Nethinims, or ministers of this house of God, it shall not be lawful to impose toll, tribute, or custom, upon them.

And thou, Ezra, after the wisdom of thy God, that is in thine hand, set magistrates and judges, which may judge all the people that are beyond the river, all such as know the laws of thy God; and teach ye them that know them not.

And whosoever will not do the law of thy God, and the law of the king, let judgment be executed speedily upon him, whether it be unto death, or to banishment, or to confiscation of goods, or to imprisonment." **Ezra 7: 1-26(kjv)**

Ezra expressed a lot of gratitude to the Lord for putting such graciousness in the king's heart.

"Blessed be the LORD God of our fathers, which hath put such a thing as this in the king's heart, to beautify the house of the LORD which is in Jerusalem:

And hath extended mercy unto me before the king, and his counsellors, and before all the king's mighty princes. And I was strengthened as the hand of the LORD my God was upon me, and I gathered together out of Israel chief men to go up with me." **Ezra 7:27-28(kjv)**

Reading the scriptures above, we can see clearly that Ezra was conscious that God had given him favour before the king, his counsellors and his mighty princes.

15. **MARY THE MOTHER OF JESUS**

It was by the favour of God that Mary became the mother of Jesus. She was definitely not the only virgin in Israel; but by divine favour God chose her to become the mother of Jesus.

"And in the sixth month the angel Gabriel was sent from God unto a city of Galilee, named Nazareth,

To a virgin espoused to a man whose name was Joseph, of the house of David; and the virgin's name was Mary.

AND THE ANGEL CAME IN UNTO HER, AND SAID, HAIL, THOU THAT ART HIGHLY FAVOURED, THE LORD IS WITH THEE: BLESSED ART THOU AMONG WOMEN.

And when she saw him, she was troubled at his saying, and cast in her mind what manner of salutation this should be.

AND THE ANGEL SAID UNTO HER, FEAR NOT, MARY: FOR THOU HAST FOUND FAVOUR WITH GOD.

And, behold, thou shalt conceive in thy womb, and bring forth a Son, and shalt call His Name JESUS.

He shall be great, and shall be called the Son of the Highest: and the Lord God shall give unto Him the throne of His father David:

And He shall reign over the house of Jacob for ever; and of His kingdom there shall be no end.

Then said Mary unto the angel, how shall this be, seeing I know not a man?

And the angel answered and said unto her, The Holy Ghost shall come upon thee, and the power of the Highest shall overshadow thee: therefore, also that holy thing which shall be born of thee shall be called the Son of God.

And, behold, thy cousin Elisabeth, she hath also conceived a son in her old age: and this is the sixth month with her, who was called barren.

For with God nothing shall be impossible.

And Mary said, Behold the handmaid of the Lord; be it unto me according to thy Word. And the angel departed from her." **Luke 1: 26-38(kjv)**

16. **JESUS CHRIST**

"And Jesus increased in wisdom and stature, and in favour with God and man." **Luke 2:52(kjv)**

17. **THE CHURCH IN JERUSALEM**

"Then they that gladly received his word were baptized: and the same day there were added unto them about three thousand souls.

And they continued stedfastly in the apostles' doctrine and fellowship, and in breaking of bread, and in prayers.

And fear came upon every soul: and many wonders and signs were done by the apostles.

And all that believed were together, and had all things common;

And sold their possessions and goods, and parted them to all men, as every man had need.

And they, continuing daily with one accord in the temple, and breaking bread from house to house, did eat their meat with gladness and singleness of heart,

Praising God, and having favour with all the people. And the Lord added to the church daily such as should be saved." **Acts 2:41-47(kjv)**

"And with great power gave the apostles witness of the resurrection of the Lord Jesus: and great grace (unmerited favour) was upon them all." **Acts 4:33(kjv)**

"Who, when he came, and had seen the grace of God, was glad, and exhorted them all, that with purpose of heart they would cleave unto the Lord." **Acts 11:23(kjv)**

18. **APOSTLE PAUL**

Paul experienced the grace of God in his life and ministry. He wrote:

"But by the grace of God I am what I am: and His grace which was bestowed upon me was not in vain; but I laboured more abundantly than they all: yet not I, but the grace of God which was with me." **1 Corinthians 15:10(kjv)**

He also wrote:

"And He said unto me, My grace is sufficient for thee: for My strength is made perfect in weakness. Most gladly therefore will I rather glory in my infirmities, that the power of Christ may rest upon me." **2 Corinthians 12:9(kjv)**

CHAPTER

BIBLE EXAMPLES OF DIVINE APPOINTMENTS CONNECTED TO DIVINE FAVOUR.

1. REBECCA MEETS ELIEZER AT THE WELL

"And he said, O LORD God of my master Abraham, I pray thee, send me good speed this day, and shew kindness unto my master Abraham.

Behold, I stand here by the well of water; and the daughters of the men of the city come out to draw water:

And let it come to pass, that the damsel to whom I shall say, let down thy pitcher, I pray thee, that I may drink; and she shall say, Drink, and I will give thy camels drink also: let the same be she that thou hast appointed for thy servant Isaac; and thereby shall I know that thou hast shewed kindness unto my master.

And it came to pass, before he had done speaking, that, behold, Rebekah came out, who was born to Bethuel, son of Milcah, the wife of Nahor, Abraham's brother, with her pitcher upon her shoulder.

And the damsel was very fair to look upon, a virgin, neither had any man known her: and she went down to the well, and filled her pitcher, and came up.

And the servant ran to meet her, and said, let me, I pray thee, drink a little water of thy pitcher.

And she said, Drink, my lord: and she hasted, and let down her pitcher upon her hand, and gave him drink.

And when she had done giving him drink, she said, I will draw water for thy camels also, until they have done drinking.

And she hasted, and emptied her pitcher into the trough, and ran again unto the well to draw water, and drew for all his camels.

And the man wondering at her held his peace, to wit whether the LORD had made his journey prosperous or not.

And it came to pass, as the camels had done drinking, that the man took a golden earring of half a shekel weight, and two bracelets for her hands of ten shekels' weight of gold;

And said, whose daughter art thou? tell me, I pray thee: is there room in thy father's house for us to lodge in?

And she said unto him, I am the daughter of Bethuel the son of Milcah, which she bares unto Nahor.

She said moreover unto him, we have both straw and provender enough, and room to lodge in.

And the man bowed down his head, and worshipped the LORD.

And he said, Blessed be the LORD God of my master Abraham, who hath not left destitute my master of his mercy and his truth: I being in the way, the LORD led me to the house of my master's brethren.

And the damsel ran, and told them of her mother's house these things." **Genesis 24: 12-28(kjv)**

2. **RACHEL MEETS JACOB AT THE WELL**

"And Jacob said unto them, my brethren, whence be ye? And they said, Of Haran are we.

And he said unto them, Know ye Laban the son of Nahor? And they said, we know him.

And he said unto them, Is he well? And they said, He is well: and, behold, Rachel his daughter cometh with the sheep.

And he said, Lo, it is yet high day, neither is it time that the cattle should be gathered together: water ye the sheep, and go and feed them.

And they said, we cannot, until all the flocks be gathered together, and till they roll the stone from the well's mouth; then we water the sheep.

And while he yet spake with them, Rachel came with her father's sheep: for she kept them.

And it came to pass, when Jacob saw Rachel the daughter of Laban his mother's brother, and the sheep of Laban his mother's brother, that Jacob went near, and rolled the stone from the well's mouth, and watered the flock of Laban his mother's brother.

And Jacob kissed Rachel, and lifted up his voice, and wept.

And Jacob told Rachel that he was her father's brother, and that he was Rebekah's son: and she ran and told her father."
Genesis 29: 4-12(kjv)

3. **JOSEPH MEETS PHARAOH'S BUTLER AND BAKER IN PRISON**

"And it came to pass after these things, that the butler of the king of Egypt and his baker had offended their lord the king of Egypt.

And Pharaoh was wroth against two of his officers, against the chief of the butlers, and against the chief of the bakers.

And he put them in ward in the house of the captain of the guard, into the prison, the place where Joseph was bound."
Genesis 40: 1-3(kjv). After meeting the butler and the baker in prison, Joseph interpreted their dreams.

"And they dreamed a dream both of them, each man his dream in one night, each man according to the interpretation of his dream, the butler and the baker of the king of Egypt, which were bound in the prison.

And Joseph came in unto them in the morning, and looked upon them, and, behold, they were sad.

And he asked Pharaoh's officers that were with him in the ward of his lord's house, saying, wherefore look ye so sadly to day?

And they said unto him, we have dreamed a dream, and there is no interpreter of it. And Joseph said unto them, do not interpretations belong to God? tell me them, I pray you.

And the chief butler told his dream to Joseph, and said to him, in my dream, behold, a vine was before me;

And in the vine were three branches: and it was as though it budded, and her blossoms shot forth; and the clusters thereof brought forth ripe grapes:

And Pharaoh's cup was in my hand: and I took the grapes, and pressed them into Pharaoh's cup, and I gave the cup into Pharaoh's hand.

And Joseph said unto him, this is the interpretation of it: The three branches are three days:

Yet within three days shall Pharaoh lift up thine head, and restore thee unto thy place: and thou shalt deliver Pharaoh's cup into his hand, after the former manner when thou wast his butler.

But think on me when it shall be well with thee, and shew kindness, I pray thee, unto me, and make mention of me unto Pharaoh, and bring me out of this house:

For indeed I was stolen away out of the land of the Hebrews: and here also have I done nothing that they should put me into the dungeon.

When the chief baker saw that the interpretation was good, he said unto Joseph, I also was in my dream, and, behold, I had three white baskets on my head:

And in the uppermost basket there was of all manner of bakemeats for Pharaoh; and the birds did eat them out of the basket upon my head.

And Joseph answered and said, this is the interpretation thereof: The three baskets are three days:

Yet within three days shall Pharaoh lift up thy head from off thee, and shall hang thee on a tree; and the birds shall eat thy flesh from off thee." **Genesis 40:5-19(kjv)**

Joseph's interpretation of the dreams of the butler and the baker came to pass. The butler promised to remember Joseph before Pharaoh, but he forgot him for two years.

"And it came to pass the third day, which was Pharaoh's birthday, that he made a feast unto all his servants: and he lifted up the head of the chief butler and of the chief baker among his servants.

And he restored the chief butler unto his butlership again; and he gave the cup into Pharaoh's hand:

But he hanged the chief baker: as Joseph had interpreted to them.

Yet did not the chief butler remember Joseph, but forgot him." **Genesis 40:20-23(kjv)**

4. JOSEPH STANDS BEFORE PHARAOH TO INTERPRET HIS DREAMS

Pharaoh had dreams which all his magicians failed to interpret. It was at this juncture that the butler whose dream Joseph had accurately interpreted, **remembered him.** The butler communicated about Joseph's abilities to interpret dreams to Pharaoh.

"Then spake the chief butler unto Pharaoh, saying, I do remember my faults this day:

Pharaoh was wroth with his servants, and put me in ward in the captain of the guard's house, both me and the chief baker:

And we dreamed a dream in one night, I and he; we dreamed each man according to the interpretation of his dream.

And there was there with us a young man, a Hebrew, servant to the captain of the guard; and we told him, and he interpreted to us our dreams; to each man according to his dream he did interpret.

And it came to pass, as he interpreted to us, so it was; me he restored unto mine office, and him he hanged." **Genesis 41:9-14(kjv)**

Joseph was called to stand before Pharaoh and he interpreted Pharaoh's dreams accurately and satisfactorily. Thus he was promptly promoted to the second most powerful position in the whole of Egypt.

"And Pharaoh said unto Joseph, Forasmuch as God hath shewed thee all this, there is none so discreet and wise as thou art.

Thou shalt be over my house, and according unto thy word shall all my people be ruled: only in the throne will I be greater than thou." **Genesis 41: 39-40(kjv)**

This was truly a divine appointment.

5. **BABY MOSES FLOATS TO DESTINY**

It was God who directed the floating of the basket which carried baby Moses to the place where Pharaoh's daughter was bathing by the river. Divine providence directed the basket to the right place at the right time. At that place God influenced Pharaoh's daughter to be compassionate to the extent of adopting Moses as her own son. The Bible says;

"And there went a man of the house of Levi, and took to wife a daughter of Levi.

And the woman conceived, and bare a son: and when she saw him that he was a goodly child, she hid him three months. And when she could not longer hide him, she took for him an ark of bulrushes, and daubed it with slime and with pitch, and put the child therein; and she laid it in the flags by the river's brink. And his sister stood afar off, to wit what would be done to him.

And the daughter of Pharaoh came down to wash herself at the river; and her maidens walked along by the river's side;

and when she saw the ark among the flags, she sent her maid to fetch it. And when she had opened it, she saw the child: and, behold, the babe wept. And she had compassion on him, and said, this is one of the Hebrews' children.

Then said his sister to Pharaoh's daughter, Shall I go and call to thee a nurse of the Hebrew women, that she may nurse the child for thee?

And Pharaoh's daughter said to her, Go. And the maid went and called the child's mother.

And Pharaoh's daughter said unto her, take this child away, and nurse it for me, and I will give thee thy wages. And the woman took the child, and nursed it. And the child grew, and she brought him unto Pharaoh's daughter, and he became her son. And she called his name Moses: and she said, because I drew him out of the water." **Exodus 2:1-10(kjv)**

6. THE DAUGHTERS OF JETHRO THE PRIEST OF MIDIAN MEET MOSES AT THE WELL.

Moses ran away from Pharaoh's wrath to the land of Midian. He arrived at a well where he met the daughters of Jethro the priest of Midian. In kindness he assisted them not knowing that amongst them one of them would later on become his wife. God provided accommodation and food also for Moses through this interaction at the well. This was a divine appointment. The Bible says;

"Now when Pharaoh heard this thing, he sought to slay Moses. But Moses fled from the face of Pharaoh, and dwelt in the land of Midian: and he sat down by a well.

Now the priest of Midian had seven daughters: and they came and drew water, and filled the troughs to water their father's flock.

And the shepherds came and drove them away: but Moses stood up and helped them, and watered their flock.

And when they came to Reuel their father, he said, how is it that ye are come so soon to day?

And they said, An Egyptian delivered us out of the hand of the shepherds, and also drew water enough for us, and watered the flock.

And he said unto his daughters, and where is he? why is it that ye have left the man? call him, that he may eat bread.

And Moses was content to dwell with the man: and he gave Moses Zipporah his daughter." **Exodus 2:15-21(kjv)**

7. SAUL MEETS SAMUEL WHILST LOOKING FOR LOST DONKEYS

Saul was looking for his father's lost donkeys. He went to various places but he could not find them. The Bible narrates the story. It says, "Now there was a man of Benjamin, whose name was Kish, the son of Abiel, the son of Zeror, the son of Bechorath, the son of Aphiah, a Benjamite, a mighty man of power.

And he had a son, whose name was Saul, a choice young man, and a goodly: and there was not among the children of Israel a goodlier person than he: from his shoulders and upward he was higher than any of the people.

And the asses of Kish Saul's father were lost. And Kish said to Saul his son, take now one of the servants with thee, and arise, go seek the asses.

And he passed through mount Ephraim, and passed through the land of Shalisha, but they found them not: then they passed through the land of Shalim, and there they were not: and he passed through the land of the Benjamites, but they found them not.

And when they were come to the land of Zuph, Saul said to his servant that was with him, Come, and let us return; lest my father leave caring for the asses, and take thought for us."
1 Samuel 9: 1-5(kjv)

Saul and his father's servant eventually agreed to go and ask for information from Samuel. Samuel was already waiting for Saul because the LORD had told him about Saul's arrival.

The prophet Samuel did not just have information about the lost donkeys which had already been found, but he had an assignment from the LORD to anoint Saul as king.

8. DAVID'S FATHER SENDS HIM TO CHECK ON THE WELFARE OF HIS BROTHERS ON THE BATTLE FRONT

David was sent by his father Jesse to check on the welfare of his brothers and also to bring to them some provisions.

"And Jesse said unto David his son, take now for thy brethren an ephah of this parched corn, and these ten loaves, and run to the camp to thy brethren;

And carry these ten cheeses unto the captain of their thousand, and look how thy brethren fare, and take their pledge." **1 Samuel 17:17-18(kjv)**

It was on this errand that David killed Goliath. His father did not send him on an assignment to kill Goliath, nor to enter into covenant with Jonathan, nor become the king's son in law and also to become a national hero. Yet all these things came to pass because David was at the right place at the right time in the centre of God's will. The Bible says:

And David said to Saul, let no man's heart fail because of him; thy servant will go and fight with this Philistine.

And Saul said to David, thou art not able to go against this Philistine to fight with him: for thou art but a youth, and he a man of war from his youth.

And David said unto Saul, thy servant kept his father's sheep, and there came a lion, and a bear, and took a lamb out of the flock:

And I went out after him, and smote him, and delivered it out of his mouth: and when he arose against me, I caught him by his beard, and smote him, and slew him.

Thy servant slew both the lion and the bear: and this uncircumcised Philistine shall be as one of them, seeing he hath defied the armies of the living God.

David said moreover, The LORD that delivered me out of

the paw of the lion, and out of the paw of the bear, He will deliver me out of the hand of this Philistine. And Saul said unto David, Go, and the LORD be with thee." **1 Samuel 17: 32-37(kjv)**

God's Word continues, and says concerning David:

And he took his staff in his hand, and chose him five smooth stones out of the brook, and put them in a shepherd's bag which he had, even in a scrip; and his sling was in his hand: and he drew near to the Philistine.

And the Philistine came on and drew near unto David; and the man that bare the shield went before him.

And when the Philistine looked about, and saw David, he disdained him: for he was but a youth, and ruddy, and of a fair countenance.

And the Philistine said unto David, Am I a dog, that thou comest to me with staves? And the Philistine cursed David by his gods.

And the Philistine said to David, come to me, and I will give thy flesh unto the fowls of the air, and to the beasts of the field.

Then said David to the Philistine, thou comest to me with a sword, and with a spear, and with a shield: but I come to thee in the name of the LORD of hosts, the God of the armies of Israel, whom thou hast defied.

This day will the LORD deliver thee into mine hand; and I will smite thee, and take thine head from thee; and I will give the carcases of the host of the Philistines this day unto the fowls of the air, and to the wild beasts of the earth; that all the earth may know that there is a God in Israel.

And all this assembly shall know that the LORD saveth not with sword and spear: for the battle is the LORD'S, and He will give you into our hands.

And it came to pass, when the Philistine arose, and came and drew nigh to meet David, that David hasted, and ran toward the army to meet the Philistine.

And David put his hand in his bag, and took thence a stone, and slang it, and smote the Philistine in his forehead, that the stone sunk into his forehead; and he fell upon his face to the earth.

So David prevailed over the Philistine with a sling and with a stone, and smote the Philistine, and slew him; but there was no sword in the hand of David.

Therefore, David ran, and stood upon the Philistine, and took his sword, and drew it out of the sheath thereof, and slew him, and cut off his head therewith. And when the Philistines saw their champion was dead, they fled.

And the men of Israel and of Judah arose, and shouted, and pursued the Philistines, until thou come to the valley, and to the gates of Ekron. And the wounded of the Philistines fell down by the way to Shaaraim, even unto Gath, and unto Ekron.

And the children of Israel returned from chasing after the Philistines, and they spoiled their tents.

And David took the head of the Philistine, and brought it to Jerusalem; but he put his armour in his tent.

And when Saul saw David go forth against the Philistine, he said unto Abner, the captain of the host, Abner, whose son is this youth? And Abner said, as thy soul liveth, O king, I cannot tell.

And the king said, enquire thou whose son the stripling is.

And as David returned from the slaughter of the Philistine, Abner took him, and brought him before Saul with the head of the Philistine in his hand.

And Saul said to him, Whose son art thou, thou young man? And David answered, I am the son of thy servant Jesse the Bethlehemite." **1 Samuel 17:40-58(kjv)**

David and Jonathan became covenant friends.

"And it came to pass, when he had made an end of speaking unto Saul, that the soul of Jonathan was knit with the soul of David, and Jonathan loved him as his own soul.

And Saul took him that day, and would let him go no more home to his father's house.

Then Jonathan and David made a covenant, because he loved him as his own soul."

1 Samuel 18:1-3(kjv)

David became very popular in Israel because of his valiant acts. He became a national hero after the slaughter of the Philistine. He had great favour in Israel.

"And David went out whithersoever Saul sent him, and behaved himself wisely: and Saul set him over the men of war, and he was accepted in the sight of all the people, and also in the sight of Saul's servants.

And it came to pass as they came, when David was returned from the slaughter of the Philistine, that the women came out of all cities of Israel, singing and dancing, to meet king Saul, with tabrets, with joy, and with instruments of musick.

And the women answered one another as they played, and said, Saul hath slain his thousands, and David his ten thousand." **1 Samuel 18:5-7(kjv)**

David became the king's son in law. All this began with his visit to the valley of Elah.

"Wherefore David arose and went, he and his men, and slew of the Philistines two hundred men; and David brought their foreskins, and they gave them in full tale to the king, that he might be the king's son in law. And Saul gave him Michal his daughter to wife."

1Samuel 18:27(kjv)

9. **RAHAB HOSTS THE SPIES SENT BY JOSHUA IN HER HOUSE IN JERICHO.**

Rahab exercised hospitality and protected the spies sent by Joshua. This was a divine appointment.

"And Joshua the son of Nun sent out of Shittim two men to spy secretly, saying, go view the land, even Jericho. And they went, and came into a harlot's house, named Rahab, and lodged there.

And it was told the king of Jericho, saying, Behold, there came men in hither to night of the children of Israel to search out the country.

And the king of Jericho sent unto Rahab, saying, bring forth the men that are come to thee, which are entered into thine house: for they be come to search out all the country.

And the woman took the two men, and hid them, and said thus, there came men unto me, but I wist not whence they were:

And it came to pass about the time of shutting of the gate, when it was dark, that the men went out: whither the men went I wot not: pursue after them quickly; for ye shall overtake them.

But she had brought them up to the roof of the house, and hid them with the stalks of flax, which she had laid in order upon the roof." **Joshua 2:1-7(kjv)**

This led to a chain of positive events which led to the blessing of her family. She and her family were promised preservation upon destruction of Jericho. After the destruction of Jericho, she and her family were assimilated into the nation of Israel.

"And they utterly destroyed all that was in the city, both man and woman, young and old, and ox, and sheep, and ass, with the edge of the sword.

But Joshua had said unto the two men that had spied out the country, go into the harlot's house, and bring out thence the woman, and all that she hath, as ye sware unto her.

And the young men that were spies went in, and brought out Rahab, and her father, and her mother, and her brethren, and all that she had; and they brought out all her kindred, and left them without the camp of Israel.

And they burnt the city with fire, and all that was therein: only the silver, and the gold, and the vessels of brass and of iron, they put into the treasury of the house of the LORD.

And Joshua saved Rahab the harlot alive, and her father's household, and all that she had; and she dwelleth in Israel even unto this day; because she hid the messengers, which Joshua sent to spy out Jericho." **Joshua 6:22-26(kjv)**

She later on got married to an Israelite of the tribe of Judah and God blessed them with a son named Boaz who became the husband of Ruth. We eventually see Rahab in the genealogy of Jesus Christ.

"And Salmon begat Boaz of Rahab; and Boaz begat Obed of Ruth; and Obed begat Jesse;

And Jesse begat David the king; and David the king begat Solomon of her that had been the wife of Urias" **Matthew 1:5-6(kjv)**

10. RUTH GOES WITH NAOMI TO BETHLEHEM, JUDAH.

Ruth the Moabitess chose to leave her home country and committed herself to go with Naomi to Bethlehem. Her popular words of commitment are recorded in God's Word:

"And Ruth said, Intreat me not to leave thee, or to return from following after thee: for whither thou goest, I will go; and where thou lodgest, I will lodge: thy people shall be my people, and thy God my God:

Where thou diest, will I die, and there will I be buried: the LORD do so to me, and more also, if ought but death part thee and me." **Ruth 1:16-17(kjv)**

She went to Bethlehem with Naomi and it was there that the LORD gave her favour in the sight of Boaz a wealthy man of Bethlehem.

"Then said Boaz unto his servant that was set over the reapers, whose damsel is this?

And the servant that was set over the reapers answered and said, it is the Moabitish damsel that came back with Naomi out of the country of Moab:

And she said, I pray you, let me glean and gather after the reapers among the sheaves: so she came, and hath continued even from the morning until now, that she tarried a little in the house.

Then said Boaz unto Ruth, Hearest thou not, my daughter? Go not to glean in another field, neither go from hence, but abide here fast by my maidens:

Let thine eyes be on the field that they do reap, and go thou after them: have I not charged the young men that they shall not touch thee? and when thou art athirst, go unto the vessels, and drink of that which the young men have drawn.

Then she fell on her face, and bowed herself to the ground, and said unto him, why have I found grace in thine eyes, that thou shouldest take knowledge of me, seeing I am a stranger?

And Boaz answered and said unto her, it hath fully been shewed me, all that thou hast done unto thy mother in law since the death of thine husband: and how thou hast left thy father and thy mother, and the land of thy nativity, and art come unto a people which thou knewest not heretofore.

The LORD recompense thy work, and a full reward be given thee of the LORD God of Israel, under whose wings thou art come to trust.

Then she said, let me find favour in thy sight, my lord; for that thou hast comforted me, and for that thou hast spoken friendly unto thine handmaid, though I be not like unto one of thine handmaidens.

And Boaz said unto her, at mealtime come thou hither, and eat of the bread, and dip thy morsel in the vinegar. And she sat beside the reapers: and he reached her parched corn, and she did eat, and was sufficed, and left.

And when she was risen up to glean, Boaz commanded his young men, saying, let her glean even among the sheaves, and reproach her not:

And let fall also some of the handfuls on purpose for her, and leave them, that she may glean them, and rebuke her not.

So she gleaned in the field until even, and beat out that she had gleaned: and it was about an ephah of barley.

And she took it up, and went into the city: and her mother in law saw what she had gleaned: and she brought forth, and gave to her that she had reserved after she was sufficed." **Ruth 2:5-18(kjv)**

Since Boaz was Ruth's kinsman redeemer; he later married her and became the heir of the estate of Elimelech.

"Therefore the kinsman said unto Boaz, Buy it for thee. So he drew off his shoe.

And Boaz said unto the elders, and unto all the people, Ye are witnesses this day, that I have bought all that was Elimelech's, and all that was Chilion's and Mahlon's, of the hand of Naomi.

Moreover, Ruth the Moabitess, the wife of Mahlon, have I purchased to be my wife, to raise up the name of the dead upon his inheritance, that the name of the dead be not cut off from among his brethren, and from the gate of his place: ye are witnesses this day.

And all the people that were in the gate, and the elders, said, we are witnesses. The LORD make the woman that is come into thine house like Rachel and like Leah, which two did build the house of Israel: and do thou worthily in Ephratah, and be famous in Bethlehem:

And let thy house be like the house of Pharez, whom Tamar bare unto Judah, of the seed which the LORD shall give thee of this young woman.

So Boaz took Ruth, and she was his wife: and when he went in unto her, the LORD gave her conception, and she bare a son.

And the women said unto Naomi, Blessed be the LORD, which hath not left thee this day without a kinsman, that his name may be famous in Israel.

And he shall be unto thee a restorer of thy life, and a nourisher of thine old age: for thy daughter in law, which loveth thee, which is better to thee than seven sons, hath born him." **Ruth 4: 8-15(kjv)**

Ruth's marriage to Boaz was a divine appointment. Ruth

is the mother of Obed by Boaz, Obed the father of Jesse, Jesse the father of King David. By divine appointment Ruth the Moabitess became the great grandmother of David. She is in the genealogy of Christ.

"And Salmon begat Boaz of Rachab; and Booz begat Obed of Ruth; and Obed begat Jesse" **Matthew 1:5(kjv)**

7

CHAPTER

————⟨⟨⟨⟩⟩⟩————

BIBLE REASONS WHY GOD'S FAVOR IS VITAL TO ALL

1. **JESUS CHRIST; THE ETERNAL SON OF GOD NEEDED FAVOUR AS A MAN ON EARTH.** The Bible says *"And Jesus increased in wisdom and stature and in favour with God and man"* **Luke2:52(kjv)** This means every Christian needs it much, much more. Since Jesus Christ whilst on earth needed Divine favour; we need it much, much, much more! **John 15:20**
2. **WITHOUT GOD'S GRACE; WHICH IS UNMERITED FAVOUR NONE OF US COULD BE SAVED.** Grace is God's unmerited favour. IT'S A FAVOUR THE BEST BEHAVIOUR OF MAN CANNOT EARN!

    The Bible says *"For by grace are ye saved through faith: and that not of yourselves: it is a gift from God: Not of works lest any man should boast."* **Ephesians 2:8-9(kjv)** In **Titus 3:5(kjv)**, the Apostle Paul also wrote: *"Not by works of righteousness which we have done, but according to His Mercy He saved us."*

3. **GOD'S UNMERITED, UNEARNED, FREELY GIVEN FAVOUR; TEACHES US TO DENY UNGODLINESS AND WORLDLY LUSTS.**

It teaches us to live soberly, righteously and godly in this present world as we look for the blessed hope and for the glorious appearing of the Great God and Saviour Jesus Christ.

The apostle Paul wrote, *"For the grace of God that bringeth salvation has appeared to all men, teaching us that denying ungodliness and worldly lusts we should live soberly righteously and godly in this present world"* **Titus 2:11-12(kjv)**

4. **THE UNMERITED, FREELY GIVEN FAVOUR OF GOD QUALIFIES AND ENABLES US TO EXCEL IN KINGDOM EXPLOITS.**

Paul wrote: *"For I am the least of the apostles, because I persecuted the church of God. But by the grace of God I am what I am: and His grace which was bestowed upon me was not in vain; but I laboured more abundantly than they all: yet not I; but the grace of God which was with me."* **1 Corinthians 15:9-10(kjv)** On just face value, others could judge us or we could even consider ourselves unqualified for the exploits in our God given assignments. **BUT GOD'S RICH GRACE IN CHRIST JESUS QUALIFIES US.**

5. **BY GOD'S UNMERITED FAVOUR (GRACE); JESUS BECAME POOR SO THAT WE WOULD BECOME RICH.**

Paul led by God's Spirit wrote: *"For you know the grace of our Lord Jesus Christ, that though He was rich, yet for your sakes He became poor, that ye through His poverty might be rich."* **2 Corinthians 8:9(kjv)**

6. **BY GOD'S UNMERITED FAVOUR THE CHRISTIAN IS ABLE TO EXPERIENCE AN OVERFLOW OF PROVISIONS SO THAT IN EVERYTHING AT ALL TIMES HE/SHE IS ABUNDANTLY SUPPLIED AND CAN ABOUND IN**

EVERY GOOD WORK! 2 Corinthians 9:8(kjv) says; *"and God is able to make all grace to abound toward you; that ye, always having all sufficiency in all things, you may abound to every good work."*
2 Corinthians 9:8(kjv)

7. **DIVINE FAVOUR CATAPULTS AND BRINGS ACCELERATION INTO GOD ORDAINED DESTINY.**

In one-day Joseph was promoted from supervising the prison to Governor of all of Egypt. God provides divine favour so that the naturally impossible He promised comes to pass. Every God given dream **NEEDS** God given favour to come to pass. So God's favour is very vital. God will punctuate the journey to the fulfilment of a God given dream with great milestones of divine favour.

Joseph's life; which I shall refer more to later is one of the best testimonies which confirm catapulting and acceleration by divine favour. He became the ruler of Egypt by divine favour. God's Word says *"And the patriarchs, becoming envious, sold Joseph into Egypt. But God was with him and delivered him out of all his troubles, and gave him favour and wisdom in the presence of Pharaoh, king of Egypt; and he made him governor over Egypt and all his house."* Acts 7:9-10(kjv)

8. **DIVINE FAVOUR CAN INFLUENCE EVEN YOUR ENEMIES TO GIVE TO YOU GIFTS OF GREAT VALUE. THIS ALSO IS SUPERNATURAL WEALTH TRANSFER.**

The children of Israel experienced it when they left Egypt. The Bible says; *"And the LORD gave the people favour in the sight of the Egyptians."* Exodus 11:3(kjv)

"And the children of Israel did according to the word of Moses; and they borrowed of the Egyptians jewels of silver, and jewels of gold, and raiment: And the LORD gave the people favour in the sight of the Egyptians, such that they

lent them such things as they required. And they spoiled the Egyptians." **Exodus 12:35-36(kjv)**

9. DIVINE FAVOUR CAN INFLUENCE HISTORIC ACQUIRING OF VALUABLE ASSETS.

God gave to the children of Israel the land of Canaan. God gave to them cities they did not build; houses they did not build; wells they did not dig; fields, vineyards, and olive yards they did not plant. According to the Bible, God had promised them,

"So it shall be, when the LORD your God brings you into the land of which He swore to your fathers, to Abraham, Isaac and Jacob, to give you large and beautiful cities which you did not build, houses full of all good things, which you did not fill, hewn-out wells you did not dig, vineyards and olive trees which you did not plant..." **Deuteronomy 6:10-11(kjv)**

10. DIVINE FAVOUR WILL GIVE YOU SUPERNATURAL VICTORIES IN BATTLES OF LIFE.

David wrote in the Psalms, *"For they did not make the land theirs by their swords, and it was not their arms which kept them safe; but Your right hand, and Your arm, and the light of Your face, because You had pleasure in them."* **Psalms 44:3(kjv)**

11. DIVINE FAVOUR CAN MOVE ONE FROM OBSCURITY TO GOD ORDAINED PROMINENCE.

We see God moving David from obscurity to prominence when God chose him to become King of Israel in the place of Saul.

"Then Samuel said to Jesse, "Are all your children here?" And he said, "There is still the youngest, and he is looking after the sheep." And Samuel said to Jesse, "Send and make him come here: for we will not take our seats till he is here."

'So he sent and brought him in. Now he was ruddy, with bright eyes, and good looking. And the Lord said, "Arise, anoint him; for this is the one!"

'Then Samuel took the horn of oil and anointed him in the midst of his brothers; and the Spirit of the Lord came upon David from that day forward. So Samuel arose and went to Ramah" 1Samuel 16: 11-13(kjv)

David the shepherd boy, also experienced this reality. The Bible says, *"And Saul sent to Jesse saying; "Let David be with me, for he is pleasing to me."'* **I Samuel 16:22(kjv)**

12. BY DIVINE FAVOUR GREAT MARRIAGES BECAME A REALITY AND CAN BECOME A REALITY TODAY.

There are substantive relationships that will take you to where you never imagined you could get to.

(i) **Rahab** the former prostitute of Jericho was married to Salmon who was of the tribe of Judah. We find Rahab in the genealogy of Jesus Christ. She experienced divine favour. The Bible says,

"Ram begot Amminadab. Amminadab begot Nahshon, and Nahshon begot Salmon. Salmon begot Boaz by Rahab, Boaz begot Obed by Ruth, Obed begot Jesse, and Jesse begot David the king. David begot Solomon" **Matthew 1:4-6(kjv)**

(ii) By divine favour **Ruth** the outcast Moabitess widow was married by the rich Bethlehemite Boaz. Boaz was a wealthy man of renown. So apart from the romantic fulfilment divine favour brought to Ruth, she also became the wife of wealthy Boaz. Divine favour moved her from gleaning the fields to owning the fields. This is not all divine favour brought to Ruth; she also became the mother of Obed who was the grandfather of King David. Ruth is in the genealogy of Christ. The Bible says, *"And Salmon became the father of Boaz, and Boaz became the father of Obed; And Obed became the father of Jesse, and Jesse became the father of David."* **Ruth 4:21-22(kjv)**

(iii) **Esther** by divine favour became the queen of Persia. The Bible says,

"And he was pleased with the girl and was kind to her; and he quickly gave her what was needed for making her clean, and the things which were hers by right, and seven servant-girls who were to be hers from the king's house: and he had her and her servant-girls moved to the best place in the women's part of the house." Esther 2:9

"Now when the turn came for Esther the daughter of Abihail, the uncle of Mordecai, who had taken her as his daughter, to go in to the king, she requested nothing but what Hegai, the king's eunuch, the custodian of the women, advised. And Esther obtained favour in the sight of all who saw her.

'So Esther was taken to King Ahasuerus into his royal palace, in the tenth month of Tebeth, in the seventh year of his reign.

The King loved Esther more than all the other women, and she obtained grace and favour in his sight more than all the virgins; so he set the royal crown upon her head and made her queen instead of Vashti." Esther 2:15-17(kjv)

13. DIVINE FAVOUR WILL EMBARRASS, DEFUSE AND DESTROY SATANIC CONSPIRACIES AGAINST YOU.

The Bible says,

"That night the king was unable to get any sleep; and he sent for the books of the records; and while some one was reading them to the king, it came out that it was recorded in the book how Mordecai had given word of the designs of Bigthana and Teresh, two of the king's servants, keepers of the door, by whom an attack on the king had been designed.

'And the king said, "What honour and reward have been given to Mordecai for this?" Then the servants who were waiting on the king said, "Nothing has been done for him."

Then the king said, "Who is in the outer room?" Now Haman had come into the outer room to get the king's authority for the hanging of Mordecai on the pillar which he had made ready for him.

'And the king's servants said to him, "See, Haman is waiting in the outer room." And the king said, "Let him come in."

'So Haman came in. And the king said to him, "What is to be done to the man whom the king has delight in honouring?" Then the thought came into Haman's mind, "Whom, more than myself, would the king have pleasure in honouring?"

And Haman, answering the king, said, "For the man whom the king has delight in honouring, let them take the robes which the king generally puts on, and the horse on which the king goes, and the crown which is on his head:

"And let the robes and the horse be given to one of the king's most noble captains, so that they may put them on the man whom the king has delight in honouring, and let him go on horseback through the streets of the town, with men crying out before him, so let it be done to the man whom the king has delight in honouring."

Then the king said to Haman, "Go quickly, and take the robes and the horse, as you have said, and do even so to Mordecai the Jew, who is seated at the king's doorway: see that you do everything as you have said."

Then Haman took the robes and the horse, and dressing Mordecai in the robes, he made him go on horseback through the streets of the town, crying out before him, 'So let it be done to the man whom the king has delight in honouring.'"
Esther 6:1-11(kjv)

14. BY DIVINE FAVOUR DISASTER, TRAGEDIES AND GENOCIDE CAN BE AVERTED.

This is confirmed in **Esther 7:1-10)kjv)** The Bible says,

'So the king and Haman came to take wine with Esther the queen. And the king said to Esther again on the second

day, while they were drinking, "What is your prayer, Queen Esther, for it will be given to you; and what is your request, for it will be done, even to the half of my kingdom."

'Then Esther the queen, answering, said, "If I have your approval, O king, and if it is the king's pleasure, let my life be given to me in answer to my prayer, and my people at my request:

"For we are given up, I and my people, to destruction and death and to be cut off. If we had been taken as men-servants and women-servants for a price, I would have said nothing, for our trouble is little in comparison with the king's loss."

Then King Ahasuerus said to Esther the queen, "Who is he and where is he who has had this evil thought in his heart?"

And Esther said, "Our hater and attacker is this evil Haman". Then Haman was full of fear before the king and the queen.

And the king in his wrath got up from the feast and went into the garden: and Haman got to his feet to make a prayer for his life to Esther the queen: for he saw that the king's purpose was evil against him.

Then the king came back from the garden into the room where they had been drinking; and Haman was stretched out on the seat where Esther was. Then the king said, "Is he taking the queen by force before my eyes in my house?" And while the words were on the king's lips, they put a cloth over Haman's face.

Then Harbonah, one of the unsexed servants waiting before the king, said, See, the pillar fifty cubits high, which Haman made for Mordecai, who said a good word for the king, is still in its place in Haman's house. Then the king said, put him to death by hanging him on it.

So Haman was put to death by hanging him on the pillar he had made for Mordecai. Then the king's wrath became less." Esther7:1-10(kjv)

15. **DIVINE FAVOUR IS LIKE A SHIELD AND GOD SURROUNDS THE RIGHTEOUS WITH IT.**

The Bible says, *'For you, Lord, will bless the righteous; with favour You will surround him as with a shield.'* **Psalm 5: 12(kjv)**

16. **DIVINE FAVOUR WILL BRING SUPERNATURAL, UNIQUE VISITATIONS FROM GOD.**

The Bible says, *'And the angel came in unto her, and said, Hail, [thou that art] highly favoured, the Lord [is] with thee: blessed [art] thou among women.'* **Luke 1:28(kjv)**

17. **THE CHURCH IN JERUSALEM THRIVED BECAUSE GOD GAVE IT FAVOUR WITH ALL THE PEOPLE.**

'Praising God, and having favour with all the people. And the Lord added to the church daily such as should be saved.' **Acts 2:47(kjv)**. It means the Church had good will and the people spoke well of it.

18. **DIVINE FAVOUR CAN INFLUENCE EVEN UNSAVED GOVERNMENT LEADERS TO SUPPORT GOD'S WORK IN CASH AND KIND.**

Even unsaved men and women; who are highly placed in governments can be influenced by God to become the administrators of His favour. In Bible times we come across heathen kings whom God used in such a fashion.

Proverbs 21:1(kjv) says, *"The king's heart is in the hand of the Lord, like the rivers of water; He turns it wherever He wishes."* The Scripture does not only refer to godly kings, but even to ungodly kings.

The heathen kings mentioned in the scriptures below were influenced by the favour of God for the fulfilment of His purposes:

(i) **PHARAOH.**

After Pharaoh promoted Joseph, he invited Jacob and his family to Egypt and gave them the land of Goshen as their dwelling place. Jacob and his family were God's covenant, chosen people. **Genesis 45:16-20(kjv)** says, *'Now the report of it was heard in Pharaoh's house saying, "Joseph's brothers have come." So it pleased Pharaoh and his servants as well. 'And Pharaoh said to Joseph, "Say to your brothers, do this: Load your animals and depart; go to the land of Canaan "Bring your father and your households and come to me; I will give you the best land of Egypt, and you will eat the fat of the land. "Now you are commanded – do this: Take carts out of the land of Egypt for your little ones and your wives; bring your father and come. "Also do not be concerned about your goods, for the best of all the land of Egypt is yours."*

After Jacob came with his family to Egypt the Bible tells us that Pharaoh gave them the best land of Egypt called Goshen to inhabit. In **Genesis 47:1-6(kjv)**, the Word of God tells us, *'Then Joseph went and told Pharaoh, and said, "My father and brothers, their flocks and their herds and all that they possess, have come from the land of Canaan; and indeed they are in the land of Goshen." 'And he took five men from among his brothers and presented them to Pharaoh. Then Pharaoh said to his brothers, "What is your occupation?" And they said to Pharaoh, "Your servants are shepherds, both we and our fathers." And they said to Pharaoh, "We have come to dwell in the land, because your servants have no pasture for their flocks, for the famine is severe in the land of Canaan. Now therefore, please let your servants dwell in the land of Goshen". Then Pharaoh spoke to Joseph, saying, "Your father and brothers have come to you. The land of Egypt is before you. Have your father and brothers dwell in the best of the land; let them dwell in Goshen. And if you know any competent men among them,*

then make them chief herdsmen over my livestock."
Genesis 47: 1-6(kjv)

In compliance with the instructions of Pharaoh King of Egypt; the Bible says concerning Joseph, *"And Joseph situated his father and brothers, and gave them a possession in the land of Egypt, in the best of the land, in the land of Rameses, as Pharaoh had commanded. 'Then Joseph provided his father, his brothers, and all his father's household with bread, according to the number in their families.'"* **Genesis 47:11-12(kjv)**

(ii) **ACHISH THE PHILISTINE KING OF GATH**

The Lord influenced the heart of Achish to be so favourable towards **David** such that he gave him the city of **Ziklag**. David only needed a temporary dwelling place; but Ziklag ended up permanently owned by the kings of Judah.

"Then David said to Achish, "If I have now found favour in your eyes, let them give me a place in some town in the country, that I may dwell there. For why should your servant dwell in the royal city with you?" So Achish gave him Ziklag that day. Therefore, Ziklag has belonged to the kings of Judah to this day." **1 Samuel 27:5-6(kjv)**

(iii)**CYRUS KING OF PERSIA**

Divine favour influenced King Cyrus to fund the rebuilding of God's temple. Cyrus made a decree in favour of the rebuilding of God's temple. He supported in cash and kind. God had availed mammoth wealth to Cyrus by his conquest of other kingdoms. He was ruling Persia which also had overthrown the empire of Babylon. The Scriptures say in **Isaiah 44:28(kjv) – Isaiah 45:1-5(kjv),**

"Who says of Cyrus, "He is my shepherd, and he shall perform all my pleasure: Saying to Jerusalem, "You shall be built" And to the temple, "Your foundation shall be laid.?" 'Thus says the LORD to His anointed, "To Cyrus, whose right hand I have held – To subdue nations

before him and loose the armour of kings, to open before him the double doors, so that the gates will not be shut: I will go before you and make the crooked places straight; I will break in pieces the gates of bronze and cut the bars of iron. I will give you treasures of darkness and hidden riches of secret places, that you may know that I, the LORD, who call you by your name, Am the God of Israel. For Jacob My servant's sake, and Israel my elect. I have even called you by your name; I have named you, though you have not known Me. I am the LORD and there is no other; There is no God besides Me. I will gird you, though you have not known Me." God fulfilled His word concerning the rebuilding of the temple through stirring the spirit of Cyrus. The Scriptures say;

"Now in the first year of Cyrus king of Persia, that the Word of the LORD by the mouth of Jeremiah might be fulfilled, the LORD stirred up the spirit of Cyrus king of Persia, that he made a proclamation throughout all his kingdom, and [put it] also in writing, saying, "Thus saith Cyrus king of Persia: The LORD God of heaven hath given me all the kingdoms of the earth; and He hath charged me to build Him a house at Jerusalem, which [is] in Judah." "Who [is there] among you of all His people? His God be with him, and let him go up to Jerusalem, which [is] in Judah, and build the house of the LORD God of Israel, (He [is] the God,) which [is] in Jerusalem. "And whosoever remaineth in any place where he sojourneth, let the men of his place help him with silver, and with gold, and with goods, and with beasts, beside the freewill offering for the house of God that [is] in Jerusalem." **Ezra 1:1-4(kjv)**

He also returned to Jerusalem all the vessels of gold and silver which Nebuchadnezzar had brought forth out of Jerusalem and put in the house of his gods. The Bible says,

"King Cyrus also brought out the articles of the house of the LORD, which Nebuchadnezzar had taken from Jerusalem and put in the temple of his gods; 'And Cyrus king of Persia brought them out by the hand of Mithredath the treasurer, and counted them out to Sheshbazzar the prince of Judah. This is the number of them: thirty gold platters, twenty-nine knives, thirty gold basins, four hundred and ten silver basins of a similar kind, and one thousand other articles. 'All the articles of gold and silver were five thousand four hundred. All these Sheshbazzar took with the captives that were brought from Babylon to Jerusalem." **Ezra 1:7-11(kjv)**

King Darius had to reinforce Cyrus' decree; by issuing another decree in favour of the rebuilding of God's temple and the offering of sacrifices unto God in Jerusalem. This was after malicious allegations had influenced the stopping of the temple rebuilding in Jerusalem. The Bible says,

"Then King Darius issued a decree, and a search was made in the archives, where the treasures were stored in Babylon. 'And at Achmetha, in the palace that is in the province of Media, a scroll was found, and in it a record was written thus: "In the first year of King Cyrus, King Cyrus issued a decree concerning the house of God at Jerusalem: "Let the house be rebuilt, the place where they offered sacrifices; and let the foundations of it be firmly laid, its height sixty cubits and its width sixty cubits, with three rows of heavy stones and one row of new timber. Let the expenses be paid from the king's treasury. Also let the gold and silver articles of the house of God, which Nebuchadnezzar took from the temple which is in Jerusalem and brought to Babylon, be restored and taken back to the temple which is in Jerusalem, each to its place; and deposit them in the house of God" — Now therefore, Tattenai, governor

of the region beyond the River, and Shethar-Boznai, and your companions the Persians who are beyond the River, keep yourselves far from there. Let the work of this house of God alone; let the governor of the Jews and the elders of the Jews build this house of God on its site. Moreover, I issue a decree as to what you shall do for the elders of these Jews, for the building of this house of God: Let the cost be paid at the king's expense from taxes on the region beyond the River; this is to be given immediately to these men, so that they are not hindered. And whatever they need — young bulls, rams, and lambs for the burnt offerings of the God of heaven, wheat, salt, wine, and oil, according to the request of the priests who are in Jerusalem — let it be given them day by day without fail, that they may offer sacrifices of sweet aroma to the God of heaven, and pray for the life of the king and his sons. Also I issue a decree that whoever alters this edict, let a timber be pulled from his house and erected, and let him be hanged on it; and let his house be made a refuse heap because of this. And may the God who causes His name to dwell there destroy any king or people who put their hand to alter it, or to destroy this house of God which is in Jerusalem. I Darius issue a decree; let it be done diligently." 'Then Tattenai, governor of the region beyond the River, Shethar-Boznai, and their companions diligently did according to what King Darius had sent. So the elders of the Jews built, and they prospered through the prophesying of Haggai the prophet and Zechariah the son of Iddo. And they built and finished it, according to the commandment of the God of Israel, and according to the command of Cyrus, Darius, and Artaxerxes king of Persia. Now the temple was finished on the third day of the month of Adar, which was in the sixth year of the reign of King Darius.' Ezra 6:1-15(kjv)

8

CHAPTER

———◇◇◇———

GOD'S PURPOSE FOR HIS FAVOUR IN YOUR LIFE.

*I*t has been said where purpose is not known, abuse is inevitable. Purpose is the reason why something exists. As I mentioned at the beginning of this book...**Divine Favour is ...from God...by God...and for God.** Every time anyone experienced divine favour in the Scriptures; there was a God reason. So we can safely conclude that there is a divine purpose which every recipient of divine favour needs to know, in order to experience the fulfilment which only comes in doing the will of God. This is a word for you dear reader.

Below I am going to list Bible examples of divine favour and its purpose. All those who received God's favour and walked in its divine purpose were greatly rewarded by God. In the Bible we have great examples of people who experienced God's favour and who also understood God's purpose for that favour. Such can be our model in the Lord on serving God's purpose for the favour He is manifesting in our lives. Below is a list of some of the saints of God who experienced His favour and served His purpose.

1. **NOAH**

The Bible says Noah found grace in the sight of the Lord, **Genesis 6:8.** God spared Noah and his family because he was a righteous man. Noah is the great grandfather of Abraham in whose lineage the Messiah was born.

Thus we see that though Noah and his family enjoyed God's favour in surviving the flood under the leadership of Noah, they served God's purposes. These are namely:

a) The preservation and perpetuation of the human race upon the earth and the replenishing of the earth. The Bible says;

   And God blessed Noah and his sons, and said unto them, be fruitful, and multiply, and replenish the earth. And the fear of you and the dread of you shall be upon every beast of the earth, and upon every fowl of the air, upon all that moveth upon the earth, and upon all the fishes of the sea; into your hand are they delivered. **Genesis 9:1-2(kjv)**

b) The preserving of a remnant in whose lineage the Messiah would be born. Abraham was a descendant of Noah and Jesus Christ is the Seed of Abraham.

   Now to Abraham and his seed were the promises made. He saith not, and to seeds, as of many; but as of one, and to thy seed, which is Christ. **Galatians 3:16(kjv)**

2. **JACOB**

God favoured Jacob over his brother Esau. Because Esau had despised his birthright, Jacob ended up getting the first born's blessing in Esau's stead. Jacob is Israel and he became the father of the twelve tribes of Israel. God's purpose of multiplying Abraham's descendants like stars has come into realization through the multiplication of the twelve tribes of Israel. God's Word says;

And, behold, the LORD stood above it, and said, I am the LORD God of Abraham thy father, and the God of Isaac: the land whereon thou liest, to thee will I give it, and to thy seed; And thy seed shall be as the dust of the earth, and thou shalt spread abroad to the west, and to the east, and to the north, and to the south: and in thee and in thy seed shall all the families of the earth be blessed. **Genesis 28:13-14(kjv)**

And God appeared unto Jacob again, when he came out of Padan-aram, and blessed him. And God said unto him, thy name is Jacob: thy name shall not be called any more Jacob, but, Israel shall be thy name: and he called his name Israel and God said unto him, I am God Almighty: be fruitful and multiply; a nation and a company of nations shall be of thee, and kings shall come out of thy loins; And the land which I gave Abraham and Isaac, to thee I will give it, and to thy seed after thee will I give the land. **Genesis 35:9-12(kjv)**

3. JOSEPH

Joseph was betrayed by his brothers into slavery in Egypt. God favoured him wherever he went. He experienced favour before his father; before Potiphar; before the keeper of the prison; and before Pharaoh the king of Egypt.

The following Scripture passages speak about favour in Joseph's life:

Now Israel loved Joseph more than all his children, because he was the son of his old age: and he made him a coat of many colors. **Genesis 37:3(kjv)**

And Joseph found grace in his sight, and he served him: and he made him overseer over his house, and all that he had he put into his hand. **Genesis 39:4(kjv)**

But the LORD was with Joseph, and showed him mercy, and gave him favor in the sight of the keeper of the prison. And the keeper of the prison committed to Joseph's hand all the prisoners that were in the prison; and whatsoever they did there, he was the doer of it. The keeper of the prison looked not to any thing that was under his hand; because the LORD was with him, and that which he did, the LORD made it to prosper. **Genesis 39:21-23(kjv)**

Thou shalt be over my house, and according unto thy word shall all my people be ruled: only in the throne will I be greater than thou. And Pharaoh said unto Joseph, See, I have set thee over all the land of Egypt. And Pharaoh took off his ring from his hand, and put it upon Joseph's hand, and arrayed him in vestures of fine linen, and put a gold chain about his neck; And he made him to ride in the second chariot which he had; and they cried before him, Bow the knee: and he made him ruler over all the land of Egypt. And Pharaoh said unto Joseph, I am Pharaoh, and without thee shall no man lift up his hand or foot in all the land of Egypt. And Pharaoh called Joseph's name Zaphnath-paaneah; and he gave him to wife Asenath the daughter of Poti-pherah priest of On. And Joseph went out over all the land of Egypt. **Genesis 41:40-45(kjv)**

And delivered him out of all his afflictions, and gave him favor and wisdom in the sight of Pharaoh king of Egypt; and he made him governor over Egypt and all his house. **Acts 7:10(kjv)**

He was promoted to become the second most powerful man in Egypt. Although Joseph personally enjoyed this prestigious post, God strategically positioned him there so that his father's house would be provided for in grand style during the period of drought. It is through this that God saved Jacob and his family from a killer drought. The following Scriptures confirm that Joseph fulfilled God's purpose in making him the governor of Egypt:

And Joseph said unto his brethren, I am Joseph; doth my father yet live? And his brethren could not answer him; for they were troubled at his presence. And Joseph said unto his brethren, come near to me, I pray you. And they came near. And he said, I am Joseph your brother, <u>whom ye sold into Egypt.</u>

Now therefore be not grieved, nor angry with yourselves, that ye sold me hither: <u>for God did send me before you to preserve life.</u> For these two years hath the famine been in the land: and yet there are five years, in the which there shall neither be earing nor harvest. <u>And God sent me before you</u> to preserve you a posterity in the earth, and to save your lives by a great deliverance. <u>So now it was not you that sent me hither, but God:</u> and he hath made me a father to Pharaoh, and lord of all his house, and a ruler throughout all the land of Egypt. Haste ye, and go up to my father, and say unto him, thus saith thy son Joseph, God hath made me lord of all Egypt: come down unto me, tarry not: And thou shalt dwell in the land of Goshen, and thou shalt be near unto me, thou, and thy children, and thy children's children, and thy flocks, and thy herds, and all that thou hast: And there will I nourish thee; for yet there are five years of famine; lest thou, and thy household, and all that thou hast, come to poverty. **Genesis 45:3-11(kjv)**

And Israel took his journey with all that he had, and came to Beer-sheba, and offered sacrifices unto the God of his father[1] Isaac. And God spoke unto Israel in the visions of the night, and said, Jacob, Jacob. And he said, here am I. And He said, I am God, the God of thy father: fear not to go down into Egypt; for I will there make of thee a great nation: I will go down with thee into Egypt; and I will also surely bring thee up again: and Joseph shall put his hand upon thine eyes. And Jacob rose up from Beer-sheba: and the sons of Israel carried Jacob their father, and their little ones, and their wives, in the wagons which Pharaoh had sent to carry him. And they took their cattle, and their goods, which they had gotten in the land of Canaan, and came into Egypt, Jacob, and all his seed with him: his sons, and his sons' sons with him, his daughters, and his sons' daughters, and all his seed brought he with him into Egypt. **Genesis 46:1-7(kjv)**

And he (Jacob) sent Judah before him unto Joseph, to direct his face unto Goshen; and they came into the land of

Goshen. And Joseph made ready his chariot, and went up to meet Israel his father, to Goshen, and presented himself unto him; and he fell on his neck, and wept on his neck a good while. And Israel said unto Joseph, now let me die, since I have seen thy face, because thou art yet alive. And Joseph said unto his brethren, and unto his father's house, I will go up, and show Pharaoh, and say unto him, my brethren, and my father's[1] house, which were in the land of Canaan, are come unto me; And the men are shepherds, for their trade hath been to feed cattle; and they have brought their flocks, and their herds, and all that they have. And it shall come to pass, when Pharaoh shall call you, and shall say, what is your occupation? That ye shall say, thy servants' trade hath been about cattle from our youth even until now, both we, and also our fathers: that ye may dwell in the land of Goshen; for every shepherd is an abomination unto the Egyptians.
Genesis 46:28-34(kjv)

Then Joseph came and told Pharaoh, and said, My father and my brethren, and their flocks, and their herds, and all that they have, are come out of the land of Canaan; and, behold, they are in the land of Goshen. And he took some of his brethren, even five men, and presented them unto Pharaoh. And Pharaoh said unto his brethren, what is your occupation? And they said unto Pharaoh, thy servants are shepherds, both we, and also our fathers. They said moreover unto Pharaoh, for to sojourn in the land are we come; for thy servants have no pasture for their flocks; for the famine is sore in the land of Canaan: now therefore, we pray thee, let thy servants dwell in the land of Goshen. And Pharaoh spoke unto Joseph, saying Thy father and thy brethren are come unto thee: The land of Egypt is before thee; in the best of the land make thy father and brethren to dwell; in the land of Goshen let them dwell: and if thou knowest any men of activity among them, then make them rulers over my cattle.
Genesis 47:1-6(kjv)

4. MOSES

Pharaoh's daughter had compassion on baby Moses when she saw him by the river. She adopted him as her own son and thus he was raised in the palace as Pharaoh's grandson.

God's purpose in all this was that in the fullness of time Moses would become His instrument for the Israelites' deliverance. God would also raise him to be the prophet who would lead Israel from Egypt to the Promised Land. God spoke to Moses in the desert of Midian whilst he was looking after the sheep of his father in law. Moses saw the burning bush which was on fire and yet it was not being consumed. Thus his attention was drawn to it and God began to speak to him. The Bible says;

And when the LORD saw that he turned aside to see, God called unto him out of the midst of the bush, and said, Moses, Moses. And he said, here am I. And he said, draw not nigh hither: put off thy shoes from off thy feet, for the place whereon thou standest is holy ground. Moreover, he said, I am the God of thy father, the God of Abraham, the God of Isaac, and the God of Jacob. And Moses hid his face; for he was afraid to look upon God. And the LORD said, I have surely seen the affliction of My people which are in Egypt, and have heard their cry by reason of their taskmasters; for I know their sorrows; And I am come down to deliver them out of the hand, of the Egyptians, and to bring them up out of that land unto a good land and a large, unto a land flowing with milk and honey; unto the place of the Canaanites, and the Hittites, and the Amorites, and the Perizzites, and the Hivites, and the Jebusites. Now therefore, behold, the cry of the children of Israel is come unto Me: and I have also seen the oppression wherewith the Egyptians oppress them. Come now therefore, and I will send thee unto Pharaoh, that thou mayest bring forth My people the children of Israel out of Egypt. **Exodus 3:4-10(kjv)**

In which time Moses was born, and was exceeding fair, and nourished up in his father's house three months: And

when he was cast out, Pharaoh's daughter took him up, and nourished him for her own son. And Moses was learned in all the wisdom of the Egyptians, and was mighty in words and in deeds. And when he was full forty years old, it came into his heart to visit his brethren the children of Israel. And seeing one of them suffer wrong, he defended him, and avenged him that was oppressed, and smote the Egyptian: For he supposed his brethren would have understood how that God by his hand would deliver them: but they understood not.
Acts 7:20-25(kjv)

Moses was faithful in fulfilling God's purpose. From Midian he went back to Egypt where God used him to bring deliverance to His people Israel.

5.   THE CHILDREN OF ISRAEL BEFORE THE EGYPTIANS

God gave the children of Israel favour in the sight of the Egyptians. When the Israelites were finally released from slavery in Egypt; they were given jewels of silver and jewels of gold plus raiment. They spoiled the Egyptians! The Bible says;

And the children of Israel did according to the word of Moses; and they borrowed of the Egyptians jewels of silver, and jewels of gold, and raiment: And the LORD gave the people favour in the sight of the Egyptians, so that they lent unto them such things as they required. And they spoiled the Egyptians. **Exodus 12:35-36(kjv)**

God blessed them with all this prosperity so that they could use it to serve Him. One of the ways they would serve Him was through giving various offerings for the building of the tabernacle in the desert. The Bible speaks about this in the following Scriptures:

And the LORD spoke unto Moses, saying Speak unto the children of Israel that they bring Me an offering: of every man that giveth it willingly with his heart ye shall take My offering. And this is the offering which ye shall take of them; gold, and silver, and brass, and blue, and purple, and scarlet, and fine linen, and goats' hair, and rams' skins dyed red, and badgers' skins, and shittim wood, Oil for the light, spices for anointing oil, and for sweet incense, Onyx stones, and stones to be set in the ephod, and in the breastplate. And let them make Me a sanctuary; that I may dwell among them. According to all that I show thee, after the pattern of the tabernacle, and the pattern of all the instruments thereof, even so shall ye make it. **Exodus 25:1-9(kjv)**

But whilst the LORD was speaking with Moses on the mountain about the building of the tabernacle, the children of Israel under the leadership of Aaron, abused the prosperity God had given them through His favour. They abused it through the making of it a golden calf. This is recorded in the whole chapter of **Exodus 32.** This brought God's wrath upon them. The sight of the golden calf and Israel's rebellion in worshipping it made Moses angry such that he casted the tables of the law God had given him out of His hands and broke them. God's judgement and wrath was executed upon the children of Israel because of this horrible sin.

Moses had to go back into the mountain to receive the tables of the law again. After he came down from the mountain the second time; he communicated to the children of Israel what God had told him about offerings for the tabernacle. This is recorded in **Exodus 35:4-19(kjv)** The children of Israel overwhelmingly gave from the prosperity which God had given them in Egypt. The Bible says;

And all the congregation of the children of Israel departed from the presence of Moses. And they came, every one whose heart stirred him up, and every one whom his spirit made willing, and they brought the LORD's offering to the work of the tabernacle of the congregation, and for all His service, and for the holy garments. And they came, both men and women, as many as were willing hearted, and brought bracelets, and earrings, and rings, and tablets, all jewels of gold: and every man that offered, offered an offering of gold unto the LORD. And every man, with whom was found blue, and purple, and scarlet, and fine linen, and goats' hair, and redskins of rams, and badgers' skins, brought them. Every one that did offer an offering of silver and brass brought the LORD's offering: and every man, with whom was found shittim wood for any work of the service, brought it. And all the women that were wise hearted did spin with their hands, and brought that which they had spun, both of blue, and of purple, and of scarlet, and of fine linen. And all the women whose heart stirred them up, in wisdom spun goats' hair. And the rulers brought onyx stones, and stones to be set, for the ephod, and for the breastplate; And spice, and oil for the light, and for the anointing oil, and for the sweet incense. The children of Israel brought a willing offering unto the LORD, every man and woman, whose heart made them willing to bring for all manner of work, which the LORD had commanded to be made by the hand of Moses. **Exodus 35:20-29(kjv)**

They gave so plentifully such that word had to be sent into the camps to stop them from bringing more.

"And they spoke unto Moses, saying, the people bring much more than enough for the service of the work, which the LORD commanded to make. And Moses gave commandment, and they caused it to be proclaimed throughout the camp, saying, let neither man nor woman make any more work for the offering of the sanctuary. So the people were restrained from bringing. For the stuff they had was sufficient for all the work to make it, and too much." **Exodus 36:5-7(kjv)**

This way, God's purpose for giving Israel prosperity was fulfilled!

6. **SAMUEL**

Samuel grew and was in favour with both God and men.

"And the child Samuel grew on, and was in favour both with the LORD, and also with men." **1 Samuel 2:26(kjv)**

Samuel was ordained of God to be God's prophet and judge of His people Israel.

"And Samuel grew and the Lord was with him, and did let none of His words fall to the ground. And all Israel from Dan even to Beersheba knew that Samuel was established to be a prophet of the LORD

"And the LORD appeared again in Shiloh for the LORD revealed Himself to Samuel in Shiloh by the Word of the Lord." **1 Samuel 3:19-21(kjv)**

7. **DAVID**

God gave David favour with Israel's men of war and all Israel. The Bible says;

"All these men of war, that could keep rank, came with a perfect heart to Hebron, to make David king over all Israel: and all the rest also of Israel were of one heart to make David king. And there they were with David three days, eating and drinking: for their brethren had prepared for them." **1 Chronicles 12:38-39(kjv)**

David served God's purpose in his generation.

"For David, after he had served God's purpose in his own generation, died and was buried with his ancestors, and so he experienced decay." **Acts 13:36(ISV)**

David was a man after God's own heart. The Bible says;

"But now thy kingdom shall not continue: the LORD hath sought Him a man after His own heart, and the LORD hath commanded him to be captain over His people, because thou hast not kept that which the LORD commanded thee." **1 Samuel 13:14(kjv)**

8. **JEWS OF KING CYRUS' DAY**

The Jews of King Cyrus' day received favour for the purpose of going back to Jerusalem to build God's house. Those who desired to go back did so. By God's favour through the king resources and support were availed to them.

"Now in the first year of Cyrus king of Persia, that the Word of the LORD by the mouth of Jeremiah might be fulfilled, the LORD stirred up the spirit of Cyrus king of Persia, that he made a proclamation throughout all his kingdom, and put it also in writing, saying, thus saith Cyrus king of Persia, The LORD God of heaven hath given me all the kingdoms of the earth; and He hath charged me to build Him an house at Jerusalem, which is in Judah.

Who is there among you of all His people? his God be with him, and let him go up to Jerusalem, which is in Judah, and build the house of the LORD God of Israel, (He is the God,) which is in Jerusalem.

And whosoever remaineth in any place where he sojourned, let the men of his place help him with silver, and with gold, and with goods, and with beasts, beside the freewill offering for the house of God that is in Jerusalem.

Then rose up the chief of the fathers of Judah and Benjamin, and the priests, and the Levites, with all them whose spirit God had raised, to go up to build the house of the LORD which is in Jerusalem.

And all they that were about them strengthened their hands with vessels of silver, with gold, with goods, and with beasts, and with precious things, beside all that was willingly offered.

Also Cyrus the king brought forth the vessels of the house of the LORD, which Nebuchadnezzar had brought forth out of Jerusalem, and had put them in the house of his gods;

Even those did Cyrus king of Persia bring forth by the hand of Mithredath the treasurer, and numbered them unto Sheshbazzar, the prince of Judah.

And this is the number of them: thirty chargers of gold, a thousand chargers of silver, nine and twenty knives,

Thirty basons of gold, silver basons of a second sort four hundred and ten, and other vessels a thousand.

All the vessels of gold and of silver were five thousand and four hundred. All these did Sheshbazzar bring up with them of the captivity that were brought up from Babylon unto Jerusalem." **Ezra 1:1-11(kjv)**

9. POST-EXILE JEWS BASED IN JERUSALEM IN KING DARIUS' DAY

The work of building God's house had been stopped because of the slander of the enemies of Jerusalem. But through God's favour King Darius had commanded a search to be done to confirm that a decree had been made by King Cyrus. The decree was located and thus king Darius by God's favour made a decree in support of it. This was God's favour to the Jews for the purpose of building God's house.

"Now therefore, if it seems good to the king, let there be search made in the king's treasure house, which is there at Babylon, whether it be so, that a decree was made of Cyrus the king to build this house of God at Jerusalem, and let the king send his pleasure to us concerning this matter." **Ezra 5: 17(kjv)**

"Then Darius the king made a decree, and search was made in the house of the rolls, where the treasures were laid up in Babylon.

And there was found at Achmetha, in the palace that is in the province of the Medes, a roll, and therein was a record thus written:

In the first year of Cyrus the king the same Cyrus the king made a decree concerning the house of God at Jerusalem, Let the house be builded, the place where they offered sacrifices, and let the foundations thereof be strongly laid; the height thereof threescore cubits, and the breadth thereof threescore cubits;

With three rows of great stones, and a row of new timber: and let the expenses be given out of the king's house:

And also let the golden and silver vessels of the house of God, which Nebuchadnezzar took forth out of the temple which is at Jerusalem, and brought unto Babylon, be restored, and brought again unto the temple which is at Jerusalem, every one to his place, and place them in the house of God.

Now therefore, Tatnai, governor beyond the river, Shetharboznai, and your companions the Apharsachites, which are beyond the river, be ye far from thence:

Let the work of this house of God alone; let the governor of the Jews and the elders of the Jews build this house of God in His place.

Moreover, I make a decree what ye shall do to the elders of these Jews for the building of this house of God: that of the king's goods, even of the tribute beyond the river, forthwith expenses be given unto these men, that they be not hindered.

And that which they have need of, both young bullocks, and rams, and lambs, for the burnt offerings of the God of heaven, wheat, salt, wine, and oil, according to the appointment of the priests which are at Jerusalem, let it be given them day by day without fail:

That they may offer sacrifices of sweet savours unto the God of heaven, and pray for the life of the king, and of his sons.

Also I have made a decree, that whosoever shall alter this word, let timber be pulled down from his house, and being set up, let him be hanged thereon; and let his house be made a dunghill for this.

And the God that hath caused His name to dwell there destroy all kings and people, that shall put to their hand to alter and to destroy this house of God which is at Jerusalem. I Darius have made a decree; let it be done with speed." Ezra **6: 1-12(kjv)**

10. EZRA

Ezra received favour before king Artaxerxes. The king made a decree very similar to the decrees of Kings Cyrus and Darius.

"This Ezra went up from Babylon; and he was a ready scribe in the law of Moses, which the LORD God of Israel had given: and the king granted him all his request, according to the hand of the LORD his God upon him.

And there went up some of the children of Israel, and of the priests, and the Levites, and the singers, and the porters, and the Nethinims, unto Jerusalem, in the seventh year of Artaxerxes the king.

And he came to Jerusalem in the fifth month, which was in the seventh year of the king.

For upon the first day of the first month began he to go up from Babylon, and on the first day of the fifth month came he to Jerusalem, according to the good hand of his God upon him.

For Ezra had prepared his heart to seek the law of the LORD, and to do it, and to teach in Israel statutes and judgments.

Now this is the copy of the letter that the king Artaxerxes gave unto Ezra the priest, the scribe, even a scribe of the words of the commandments of the LORD, and of His statutes to Israel.

Artaxerxes, king of kings, unto Ezra the priest, a scribe of the law of the God of heaven, perfect peace, and at such a time.

I make a decree, that all they of the people of Israel, and of his priests and Levites, in my realm, which are minded of their own freewill to go up to Jerusalem, go with thee.

Forasmuch as thou art sent of the king, and of his seven counsellors, to enquire concerning Judah and Jerusalem, according to the law of thy God which is in thine hand;

And to carry the silver and gold, which the king and his counsellors have freely offered unto the God of Israel, whose habitation is in Jerusalem,

And all the silver and gold that thou canst find in all the province of Babylon, with the freewill offering of the people, and of the priests, offering willingly for the house of their God which is in Jerusalem:

That thou mayest buy speedily with this money bullocks, rams, lambs, with their meat offerings and their drink offerings, and offer them upon the altar of the house of your God which is in Jerusalem.

And whatsoever shall seem good to thee, and to thy brethren, to do with the rest of the silver and the gold, that do after the will of your God.

The vessels also that are given thee for the service of the house of thy God, those deliver thou before the God of Jerusalem.

And whatsoever more shall be needful for the house of thy God, which thou shalt have occasion to bestow, bestow it out of the king's treasure house.

And I, even I Artaxerxes the king, do make a decree to all the treasurers which are beyond the river, that whatsoever Ezra the priest, the scribe of the law of the God of heaven, shall require of you, it be done speedily,

Unto a hundred talents of silver, and to a hundred measures of wheat, and to a hundred baths of wine, and to a hundred baths of oil, and salt without prescribing how much.

Whatsoever is commanded by the God of heaven, let it be diligently done for the house of the God of heaven: for why should there be wrath against the realm of the king and his sons?

Also we certify you, that touching any of the priests and Levites, singers, porters, Nethinims, or ministers of this house of God, it shall not be lawful to impose toll, tribute, or custom, upon them.

And thou, Ezra, after the wisdom of thy God, that is in thine hand, set magistrates and judges, which may judge all the people that are beyond the river, all such as know the laws of thy God; and teach ye them that know them not.

And whosoever will not do the law of thy God, and the law of the king, let judgment be executed speedily upon him, whether it be unto death, or to banishment, or to confiscation of goods, or to imprisonment." **Ezra 7:6-26(kjv)**

Apart from the resources Ezra and the Jews who would

travel with him to Jerusalem would carry; Ezra's ministry would be very essential in Jerusalem. This is because Ezra was a diligent and excellent student, doer and teacher of the law of God. The Bible says:

"For Ezra had prepared his heart to seek the law of the LORD, and to do it, and to teach in Israel statutes and judgments." **Ezra 7:10(kjv)**

The post-exile Jews in Jerusalem needed someone to teach them the law of God so that they would not sin against their God.

11. NEHEMIAH

God gave Nehemiah favour in the sight of king Artaxerxes. God's purpose for giving him that favour was to enable him to build the walls of Jerusalem. God's Word says,

"And I said unto the king, if it please the king, and if thy servant has found favour in thy sight, that thou wouldest send me unto Judah, unto the city of my fathers' sepulchres that I may build it." **Nehemiah 2:5(kjv)**

Nehemiah was given leave by King Artaxerxes to go to Jerusalem to build the walls.

"And the king granted me, according to the good hand of my God upon me." **Nehemiah 2:8.**

12. ESTHER

Esther was selected above all the beautiful women of the Persian Kingdom to become the Queen. God showed His favour so that He could save the Israelites from being annihilated. The Bible says,

"Now when the turn of Esther the daughter of Abihail the uncle of Modercai who had taken her for his daughter, was come to go in unto the king, she required nothing but what Hegai the king's chamberlain, the keeper of the women, appointed. And Esther obtained favour in the sight of all them that looked upon her. "So Esther was taken unto king

Ahasuerus into his house royal in the tenth month, which is the month Tebeth, in the seventh year of his reign. And the king loved Esther above all the women, and she obtained grace and favour in his sight more than all the virgins: so that he set the royal crown upon her head, and made her queen instead of Vashti. Then the king made a great feast unto all his princes and his servants, even Esther's feast; and he made a release to the provinces, and gave gifts, according to the state of the king". **Esther 2:15-18(kjv)**

Mordecai spells out the purpose of God's favour upon Esther in this verse,

"For if thou altogether holdest thy peace at this time, then shall there 3enlargement and deliverance arise to the Jews from another place; but thou and thy father's house shall be destroyed: and who knoweth whether thou art come to the kingdom for such a time as this." **Esther 4:14(kjv)**

13. **MORDECAI**

Mordecai experienced God's favour. He was given abnormal promotion. This is the promotion Haman the enemy of the Jews had recommended to King Ahasuerus as appropriate for the man who pleased the king. Haman thought he was the man the King was making reference to when he asked for advice on what should be done for the man who pleased the king. The following were Haman's suggestions which the king immediately told Haman to carry out on behalf of the king:

And the king said, who is in the court? Now Haman was come into the outward court of the king's house, to speak unto the king to hang Mordecai on the gallows that he had prepared for him. And the king's servants said unto him, Behold, Haman standeth in the court. And the king said, let him come in. So Haman came in. And the king said unto him, what shall be done unto the man whom the king delighteth to honor? Now Haman thought in his heart, to whom would the king delight to do honor more than to myself? And Haman answered the king, For the man whom the king delighteth to honor, Let the royal apparel be brought which the king useth to wear, and the horse that the king rideth upon, and the crown royal which is set upon his head: And let this apparel and horse be delivered to the hand of one of the king's most noble princes, that they may array the man withal whom the king delighteth to honor, and bring him on horseback through the street of the city, and proclaim before him, Thus shall it be done to the man whom the king delighteth to honor. Then the king said to Haman, make haste, and take the apparel and the horse, as thou hast said, and do even so to Mordecai the Jew, that sitteth at the king's gate: let nothing fail of all that thou hast spoken. Then took Haman the apparel and the horse, and arrayed Mordecai, and brought him on horseback through the street of the city, and proclaimed before him, thus shall it be done unto the man whom the king delighteth to honor. **Esther 6:4-11(kjv)**

And Mordecai went out from the presence of the king in royal apparel of blue and white, and with a great crown of gold, and with a garment of fine linen and purple: and the city of Shushan rejoiced and was glad. The Jews had light, and gladness, and joy, and honor. And in every province, and in every city, whithersoever the king's commandment and his decree came, the Jews had joy and gladness, a feast and a good day. And many of the people of the land became Jews; for the fear of the Jews fell upon them. **Esther 8:15-17(kjv)**

Mordecai was committed to the welfare of the Jews. He was instrumental in their deliverance from the conspiracy of Haman. God turned the harm Mordecai's enemies meant against him for good. Mordecai found favour in the eyes of the King and became powerful and great. God's master plan for delivering the Jews involved Mordecai by virtue of his close relationship to Queen Esther. Mordecai became very great indeed as illustrated in the verse below. In his greatness as I mentioned before, he sought the welfare of the Jews. God's Word says:

"For Mordecai the Jew was next unto king Ahasuerus, and great among the Jews, and accepted of the multitude of his brethren, seeking the welfare of his people, and speaking peace to all his seed." **Esther 10:3(kjv)**

14. DANIEL AND THE THREE HEBREW BOYS

Daniel the Jew, and the three Hebrew boys were given positions of high rank by both Babylonian and Persian Kings because of their excellent spirit that was given to them by God. Their refusal to worship the man made god and their steadfastness in worshipping their God earned them God's favour. This favour protected them in the fiery furnace and also in the lion's den, and also caused their promotion. God was therefore able to show His might while at the same time preserved Daniel to tell the great prophecy. The Bible about this says;

"Then Nebuchadnezzar spake, and said, Blessed be the God of Shadrach, Meshach, and Abednego, who hath sent His angel, and delivered His servants that trusted in Him, and have changed the king's word, and yielded their bodies, that they might not serve nor worship any god, except their own God. Therefore, I make a decree, that every people, nation, and language, which speak anything amiss against the God of Shadrach, Meshach, and Abednego, shall be cut in pieces, and their houses shall be made a dunghill: because there is no other God that can deliver after this sort. Then the king promoted Shadrach, Meshach, and Abednego, in the province of Babylon." **Daniel 3:28-30(kjv)**

15. CYRUS KING OF PERSIA

God favoured Cyrus the Persian King to become rich and powerful so that He could allow and fund the Jews in his empire to go home to Jerusalem and rebuild God's House. He was also able to give provisions for the Israelites to be able to rebuild God's House. The Bible reads;

"That saith of Cyrus, He is my shepherd, and shall perform all My pleasure: even saying to Jerusalem, thou shalt be built; and to the temple, thy foundation shall be laid.

"Thus saith the Lord to His anointed, to Cyrus, whose right hand I have holden, to subdue nations before him; and I will loose the loins of kings, to open before him the two leaved gates; and the gates shall not be shut; I will go before thee, and make the crooked places straight; I will break in pieces the gates of brass, and cut in sunder the bars of iron: And I will give thee the treasures of darkness, and hidden riches of secret places, that thou mayest know that I, the Lord, which call thee by thy name, am the God of Israel. For Jacob My servant's sake, and Israel Mine elect, I have even called thee by thy name; I have surnamed thee, though thou hast not known Me. I am the Lord, and there is none else, there is no God beside Me; I girded thee, though thou hast not known Me:" Isaiah 44:28(kjv) – 45:1-5(kjv)

This prophetic Word from God through Isaiah was fulfilled. This is recorded in the book of Ezra.

"Now in the first year of Cyrus king of Persia, that the Word of the LORD by the mouth of Jeremiah might be fulfilled, the LORD stirred up the spirit of Cyrus king of Persia, that he made a proclamation throughout all his kingdom, and put it also in writing, saying, thus saith Cyrus king of Persia, The Lord God of heaven hath given me all the kingdoms of the earth; and he hath charged me to build Him a house at Jerusalem, which is in Judah. Who is there among you of all His people? his God be with him, and let him go up to Jerusalem, which is in Judah, and build the house of the Lord God of Israel, (He is the God,) which is in Jerusalem.

And whosoever remaineth in any place where he sojourneth, let the men of his place help him with silver, and with gold, and with goods, and with beasts, beside the freewill offering for the house of God that is in Jerusalem." Ezra 1:1-4(kjv)

16. EZRA AND THE JEWS

The Jews found favour in the eyes of Artaxerxes who allowed the Israelites to go to Jerusalem so that they could make an offering unto the LORD He also gave them provisions of gold and silver which were used to serve in the house of the LORD including bullocks, rams and lambs for the offerings.

King Artaxerxes's commitment to carry out God's favour on the Jews is shown in this passage of Scripture;

"I make a decree, that all they of the people of Israel, and of his priests and levites, in my realm, which are minded of their own freewill to go up to Jerusalem, go with thee. Forasmuch as thou art sent of the king, and of his seven counsellors, to enquire concerning Judah and Jerusalem, according to the law of thy God which is in thine hand; And to carry the silver and gold, which the king and his counsellors have freely offered unto the God of Israel, whose habitation is in Jerusalem, And all the silver and gold that thou canst find in all the province of Babylon, with the freewill offering of the people, and of the priests, offering willingly for the house of their God which is in Jerusalem: That thou mayest buy speedily with this money bullocks, rams, lambs, with their meat offerings, and offer them upon the altar of the house of your God which is in Jerusalem. And whatsoever shall seem good to thee, and to thy brethren, to do with the rest of the silver and the gold, that do after the will of your God. The vessels also that are given thee for the service of the house of thy God, those deliver thou before the God of Jerusalem. And whatsoever more shall be needful for the house of thy God, which thou shalt have occasion to bestow, bestow it out of the king's treasure house. And I, even I Artaxerxes the king, do make a decree to all the treasurers which are beyond the river, that whatsoever Ezra the priest, the scribe of the law of the God of heaven, shall require of you, it be done speedily" **Ezra 7:13-21(kjv)**

17. **MARY THE MOTHER OF JESUS**

Mary experienced divine favour so that the Son of God Jesus would be born into the world. This favour did not come to her for the sake of her own personal prestige but because of God's agenda of bringing His Son into the world through a virgin.

This was to fulfil what God spoke through the prophet Isaiah,

"Therefore the Lord Himself shall give you a sign; Behold, a virgin shall conceive, and bear a Son, and shall call His Name Immanuel." **Isaiah 7:14(kjv)**

"And in the sixth month the angel Gabriel was sent from God unto a city of Galilee, named Nazareth,

To a virgin espoused to a man whose name was Joseph, of the house of David; and the virgin's name was Mary.

AND THE ANGEL CAME IN UNTO HER, AND SAID, HAIL, THOU THAT ART HIGHLY FAVOURED, THE LORD IS WITH THEE: BLESSED ART THOU AMONG WOMEN.

And when she saw him, she was troubled at his saying, and cast in her mind what manner of salutation this should be.

AND THE ANGEL SAID UNTO HER, FEAR NOT, MARY: FOR THOU HAST FOUND FAVOUR WITH GOD.

And, behold, thou shalt conceive in thy womb, and bring forth a Son, and shalt call His Name JESUS.

He shall be great, and shall be called the Son of the Highest: and the Lord God shall give unto Him the throne of His father David:

And He shall reign over the house of Jacob for ever; and of His kingdom there shall be no end.

Then said Mary unto the angel, how shall this be, seeing I know not a man?

And the angel answered and said unto her, The Holy Ghost shall come upon thee, and the power of the Highest shall overshadow thee: therefore, also that holy thing which shall be born of thee shall be called the Son of God.

And, behold, thy cousin Elisabeth, she hath also conceived

a son in her old age: and this is the sixth month with her, who was called barren.

For with God nothing shall be impossible.

And Mary said, Behold the handmaid of the Lord; be it unto me according to Thy Word. And the angel departed from her." **Luke 1: 26-38(kjv)**

18. JESUS CHRIST

"And Jesus increased in wisdom and stature, and in favour with God and man." **Luke 2:52(kjv)**

19. THE CHURCH IN JERUSALEM

Every church needs God's favour in order for it to fulfil its God given purpose. The church in Jerusalem had divine favour and it experienced explosive growth.

"Then they that gladly received his Word were baptized: and the same day there were added unto them about three thousand souls.

And they continued steadfastly in the apostles' doctrine and fellowship, and in breaking of bread, and in prayers.

And fear came upon every soul: and many wonders and signs were done by the apostles.

And all that believed were together, and had all things common;

And sold their possessions and goods, and parted them to all men, as every man had need.

And they, continuing daily with one accord in the temple, and breaking bread from house to house, did eat their meat with gladness and singleness of heart,

Praising God, AND HAVING FAVOUR WITH ALL THE PEOPLE. And the Lord added to the church daily such as should be saved." **Acts 2:41-47(kjv)**

"And with great power gave the apostles witness of the resurrection of the Lord Jesus: and great grace (unmerited favour) was upon them all." **Acts 4:33(kjv)**

The church at Antioch walked also in the favour of God. When Barnabas arrived, he saw tangible evidence of God's grace upon the church and he exhorted the brethren.

"Who, when he came, and had seen the grace of God, was glad, and exhorted them all, that with purpose of heart they would cleave unto the Lord." **Acts 11:23(kjv)**

20. **APOSTLE PAUL**

The grace of God in Paul was not in vain. By this grace Paul says he laboured more abundantly than the rest of the apostles.

"But by the grace of God I am what I am: and His grace which was bestowed upon me was not in vain; but I laboured more abundantly than they all: yet not I, but the grace of God which was with me." **1 Corinthians 15:10(kjv)**

By God's grace in Christ Jesus, Paul also managed to endure hardships and persecutions which under normal circumstances would cause a person to give up.

"And He said unto me, My grace is sufficient for thee: for My strength is made perfect in weakness. Most gladly therefore will I rather glory in my infirmities, that the power of Christ may rest upon me." **2 Corinthians 12:9(kjv)**

He was able to run his God given race to the finish line successfully. *"I have fought a good fight, I have finished my course, I have kept the faith."* **2 Timothy 4:7(kjv)**

9

CHAPTER

LIST OF SCRIPTURES
ON DIVINE FAVOUR
TO MEDITATE ON

1. **Genesis 4:4** (NIV) *"But Abel brought fat portions from some of the firstborn of his flock. The LORD looked with FAVOUR on Abel and his offering."*
2. **Genesis 6:8** (AMPLIFIED) *"But Noah found grace (FAVOUR) in the eyes of the Lord."*
3. **Genesis 12:2** (AMPLIFIED) *"And I will make of you a great nation, and I will bless you [with abundant increase of FAVOURS] and make your name famous and distinguished, and you will be a blessing [dispensing good to others]."*
4. **Genesis 18:3-5** (AMPLIFIED) *"And said, my lord, if now I have found FAVOUR in your sight, do not pass by your servant, I beg you. Let a little water be brought, and you may wash your feet and recline and rest yourselves under the tree. And I will bring a morsel (mouthful) of bread to refresh and sustain your hearts before you go on any further – for that is why you have come to your servant. And they replied, do as you have said."*

5. **Genesis 39:2-6** (AMPLIFIED) *"The Lord was with Joseph, so he became a successful man. And he was in the house of his master, the Egyptian. Now his master saw that the Lord was with him and how the Lord caused all that he did to prosper in his hand. So Joseph pleased [Potiphar] and found FAVOUR in his sight, and he served him. And [his master] made him supervisor over his house and he put all that he had in his charge. From the time that he made him supervisor in his house and all that he had, the Lord blessed the Egyptian's hose for Joseph's sake; and the Lord's blessing was on all that he had in the house and in the field. And [Potiphar] let all that he had in Joseph's charge and paid no attention to anything he had except the food he ate. Now Joseph was an attractive person and fine looking."*

6. **Genesis 39:20-23** (AMPLIFIED) *"And Joseph's master took him and put him in the prison, a place where the state prisoners were confined; so he was there in the prison. But the Lord was with Joseph, and showed him mercy and loving-kindness and gave him FAVOUR in the sight of the warden of the prison. And the warden of the prison committed to Joseph's care all the prisoners who were in the prison; and whatsoever was done there, he was in charge of it. The prison warden paid no attention to anything that was in [Joseph's] charge, for the Lord was with him and made whatever he did to prosper."*

7. **Exodus 3:21**(KJV) *"And I will give this people FAVOUR in the sight of the Egyptians: and shall come to pass, that, when ye go, ye shall not go empty".*

8. **Exodus 11:2-3** (AMPLIFIED) *"Speak now in the hearing of the people, and let every man solicit and ask of his neighbour, and every woman of her neighbour, jewels of silver and jewels of gold. And the Lord gave the people FAVOUR in the sight of the Egyptians. Moreover, the man Moses was exceedingly great in the land of Egypt, in the sight of Pharaoh's servants and the people."*

9. **Exodus 12:35-36** (AMPLIFIED) *"The Israelites did according to the word of Moses; and they [urgently] asked of the Egyptians jewels of silver and of gold, and clothing. The Lord gave the people FAVOUR in the sight of the Egyptians, so that they gave them what they asked. And they stripped the Egyptians [of those things]."*

10. **Exodus 33:11-13** (AMPLIFIED) *"And the Lord spoke to Moses face to face, as a man speaks to his friend. Moses returned to the camp, but his minister Joshua son of Nun, a young man, did not depart from the (temporary prayer) tent. Moses said to the Lord, See, you say to me, bring up this people, but You have not let me know whom You will send with me. Yet You said, I know you by name and you have also found FAVOUR in My sight. Now therefore, I pray You, if I have find FAVOUR in Your sight, show me now Your way, that I may know You [progressively become more deeply and intimately acquainted with You, perceiving and recognizing and understanding more strongly and clearly] and that I may find FAVOUR in Your sight. And [Lord, do] consider that this nation is Your people."*

11. **Exodus 34:9-10** (AMPLIFIED) *"And He said, if now I have found FAVOUR and loving-kindness in Your sight, O Lord, let the Lord, I pray You, go in the midst of us, although it is stiff-necked people, and pardon our iniquity and our sin, and take us for Your inheritance. And the Lord said, Behold, I lay down [afresh the terms of the mutual agreement between Israel and Me] a covenant. Before all your people I will do marvels (wonders, miracles) such as have not been wrought or created in all the earth or in any nation; and all the people among whom you are shall see the work of the Lord; for it is a terrible thing [fearful and full of awe] that I will do with you."*

12. **Leviticus 26:1-9** (NIV) *"'DO NOT make idols or set up an image or a sacred stone for yourselves, and do not place a carved stone in your land to bow down before it. I*

am the Lord your God. "'Observe my Sabbaths and have reverence for My sanctuary. I am the Lord. "'If you follow My decrees and are careful to obey My commands, I send you rain in its season, and the ground will yield its crops and the trees of the field their fruit. Your threshing will continue until grape harvest and the grape harvest will continue until planting, and you will eat all the food you want and live in safety in your land. "'I will grant peace in the land, and you will lie down and no one will make you afraid. I will move savage beasts from the land, and then sword will not pass through your country. You will pursue your enemies, and they will fall by the sword before you. Five of you will chase a hundred, and a hundred of you will chase ten thousand, and your enemies will fall by the sword before you. I will look on you with FAVOUR and make you fruitful and increase your numbers, and I will keep My covenant with you.'"

13. **Numbers 6:24-26** (AMPLIFIED) *"The Lord bless you and watch, guard, and keep you; The Lord makes His face shine upon and enlighten you and be gracious (kind, merciful, and giving FAVOUR) to you; The Lord lifts up His [approving] countenance upon you and give you peace (tranquillity of heart and life continually)."*

14. **Judges 6:17-21**(AMPLIFIED) *"Gideon said to Him, if now I have found FAVOUR in your sight, then show me a sign that it is You Who talks with me. Do not leave here, I pray you, until I return to You and bring my offering and set it before You. And He said I will wait until you return. Then Gideon went in and prepared a kid and unleavened cakes of an ephah of flour. The meat he put in a basket and the broth in a pot, and brought them to Him under the oak and presented them. And the Angel of God said to him, Take the meat and unleavened cakes, and lay them on this rock and pour the broth over them. And he did so. Then the Angel of the Lord reached out the tip of the staff that was*

in His hand, and touched the meat and the unleavened cakes, and there flared up fire from the rock and consumed the meat and the unleavened cakes. Then the Angel of the Lord vanished from the sight."

15. **Ruth 2:8-13**(AMPLIFIED) *"Then Boaz said to Ruth, listen, my daughter, do not go to glean in another field or leave this one, but stay here close by my maidens. Watch which field they reap, and follow them. Have I not charged the young men not to molest you? And when you are thirsty, go to the vessels and drink what the young men have drawn. Then she fell on her face, bowing to the ground, and said to him, why have I found favour in your eyes that you should notice me, when I am a foreigner? And Boaz said to her, I have been made fully aware of all you have done for your mother in-law since the death of your husband, and how you have left your father and mother and the land of your birth and have come to a people unknown to you before. The LORD recompense you for what you have done, and a full reward be given to you by the LORD, the God of Israel, under whose wings have come to take refuge! `Then she said, let me find favour in your sight, my lord. For you have comforted me and have spoken to the heart of your maidservant, though I am not as one of your maidservants."*

16. **1 Samuel 2:26** (KJV) *"and the child Samuel grew on, and was in FAVOUR both with the LORD, and also with men."*

17. **2 Samuel 9:1** (KJV) *"AND DAVID said, is there yet any that is left of the house of Saul, that I show him kindness for Jonathan's sake?"*

18. **Esther 2:15** (AMPLIFIED) *"Now when the turn of Esther the daughter of Abihail, the uncle of Mordecai who had taken her as his own daughter, had come to go in to the king, she required nothing but what Hegai the king's attendant, the keeper of the women, suggested. And Esther won FAVOUR in the sight of all who saw her."*

19. **Esther 7:3** (KJV) *"Then Esther the queen answered and said, if I have found favour in thy sight, o king, and if it pleases the king, let my life be given me at my petition, and my people at my request."*

20. **Job 10:12** (AMPLIFIED) *"You have granted me life and favour, and Your providence has preserved my spirit."*

21. **Job 33:26** (KJV) *"He shall pray unto God, and He will be favourable unto him: and He shall see His face with joy: for He will render unto men His righteousness."*

22. **Psalms 5:12** (KJV) *"For thou, Lord, wilt bless the righteous; with favour wilt thou compass him as with a shield."*

23. **Psalm 30:5;7** (KJV) *"For His anger endureth but a moment; in His favour is life: weeping may endure for night, but joy cometh in the morning. LORD, by Thy favour Thou has made my mountain to stand strong: Thou didst hide Thy face, and I was troubled."*

24. **Psalm 41:11** (AMPLIFIED) *"By this I know that You favour and delight in me, because my enemy does not triumph over me."*

25. **Psalm 44:3** (AMPLIFIED) *"For they got not the land [of Canaan] in possession by their own sword, neither did their own arm save them; but Your right hand and Your arm and light of your countenance [did it], because You were favourable toward and did delight in them."*

26. **Psalm 45:12**(KJV) *"And the daughter of Tyre shall be there with a gift; even the rich among the people shall entreat thy favour."*

27. **Psalm 80:3** (AMPLIFIED) *"Restore us again, O God; and cause Your face to shine [in pleasure and approval on us], and we shall be saved!"*

28. **Psalm 80:19** (AMPLIFIED) *"Restore us, O LORD God of hosts; cause Your face to shine [in pleasure, approval. and favour on us], and we shall be saved!"*

29. **Psalm 85:1-3** (KJV) *"LORD, THOU has been favourable unto Thy land: Thou has brought back the captivity of*

Jacob. Thou hast forgiven the inequity of Thy people; Thou hast covered all their sin. Thou hast taken away all Thy wrath: Thou hast turned Thyself from the fierceness of Thine anger."

30. **Psalm 89:17** (KJV) *"For Thou art the glory of their strength: and in Thy favour our horn shall be exalted."*

31. **Psalm 90:17** (AMPLIFIED) *"And let the beauty and delightfulness and favour of the Lord our God be upon us; confirm and establish the work of our hands- yes, the work of our hands, confirm and establish it."*

32. **Psalm 102:13** (KJV) *"Thou shalt arise, and have mercy upon Zion: for the time to favour her, yea, the set time, is come."*

33. **Proverbs 3:3-4**(KJV) *"let not mercy and truth forsake thee: bind them about thy neck; write them upon the table of thine heart: So shalt thou find favour and good understanding in the sight of God and man."*

34. **Proverbs 8:35** (AMPLIFIED) *"for whoever finds me [Wisdom) finds life and draws forth and obtains favour from the Lord."*

35. **Proverbs 12:2** (AMPLIFIED) *"A good man obtains favour from the LORD, but a man of wicked devices He condemns."*

36. **Proverbs 13:15** (KJV) *"Good understanding giveth favour: but the way of transgressors is hard."*

37. **Proverbs 18:22** (KJV) *"whosoever findeth a wife findeth a good thing, and obtaineth favour of the LORD,"*

38. **Proverbs 19:6** (AMPLIFIED) *"Many will entreat the favour of a liberal man, and every man is a friend of him who gives gifts."*

39. **Isaiah 30:18** (AMPLIFIED) *"and therefore the Lord [earnestly] waits [expecting, looking, and longing] to be gracious to you; and therefore He lifts Himself up, that He may have mercy on you and show loving-kindness to you. For the LORD is a God of justice. Blessed (happy,*

fortunate, to be envied) are all those who [earnestly] wait for Him, who expect and look and long for Him [for His victory, His favour, His love, His peace, His joy, and His matchless, unbroken companionship]!"

40. **Isaiah 60:10-11** (AMPLIFIED) *"Foreigners shall build up your walls, and their kings shall minister to you; for in My wrath l smote you, but in My favour, pleasure, and goodwill l have had mercy, love and pity for you. And your gates shall be open continually, they shall not be shut day or night that men may bring to you the wealth of the nations- and their kings led in procession [your voluntary captives].*

41. **Isaiah 61:1-2**(NIV) *"THE SPIRIT of the Sovereign Lord is upon Me; because the LORD has anointed Me to preach good news to the poor; He has send Me to bind up the broken hearted, to proclaim freedom for the captives and release from darkness for the prisoners, to proclaim the year of the Lord's favour and the day of vengeance of our God, to comfort all who mourn."*

42. **Daniel 1:8-9** (KJV) *"But Daniel purposed in his heart, that he would not defile himself with the portion of the king's meat, nor with the wine which he drank: therefore, he requested of the prince of the eunuchs that he might not defile himself. Now God had brought Daniel in favour and tender love with the prince of the eunuchs."*

43. **Luke 1:28-38** (KJV) *"And the angel came in unto her, and said, Hail, thou art highly favoured, the Lord is with thee: blessed art thou among women. And when she saw him, she was troubled at his saying, and cast in her mind what manner of salutation this should be. And the angel said unto her, Fear not Mary for thou hast found favour with God. And behold, thou shall conceive in thy womb and bring forth a Son, and shalt call His name JESUS. He shall be great, and shall be called the Son of the Highest: and the Lord God shall give unto Him the throne of His father David. And He shall reign over the house of Jacob*

forever, and of His kingdom there shall be no end. Then said Mary unto the angel, how shall this be, seeing that I know not a man? And the angel answered and said unto her, The Holy Ghost shall come upon thee, and the power of the Highest shall overshadow thee: therefore, also that holy thing which shall be born of thee shall be called the Son of God. And, behold, thy cousin Elizabeth, she hath also conceived a son in her old age: and this is the sixth month with her, who was called barren. For with God nothing shall be impossible. And Mary said, Behold the handmaid of the Lord; be it unto me according thy Word. And the angel departed from her."

44. **Luke 2:14** (AMPLIFIED) *"Glory to God in the highest [heaven], and on earth peace among men with whom He is well pleased [men of goodwill, of His favour]."*

45. **Luke 2:52** (KJV) *"And Jesus increased in wisdom and stature and in favour with God and man."*

46. **Luke 4:18-19** (KJV) *"The Spirit of the Lord [is] upon Me, because He has anointed Me [the Anointed one, the Messiah] to preach the Good News (the Gospel) to the poor, He has sent Me to announce release to the captives and recovery of sight to the blind, to send forth as delivered those who are oppressed [who are down trodden, bruised, crushed, and broken down by calamity], To proclaim the accepted and acceptable year of the Lord [the day when salvation and free favours of God profusely abound]."*

47. **Acts 2:47** (AMPLIFIED) *"constantly praising God and being in favour and goodwill with all people; and the Lord kept adding [to their number] daily those who were being saved [from spiritual death]."*

48. **Acts 7:9-10** (KJV) *"And the patriarchs, moved with envy, sold Joseph into Egypt: but God was with him, and delivered him out of all his afflictions, and gave him favour and wisdom in the sight of Pharaoh king of Egypt; and he made him governor over Egypt and all his house."*

49. **Acts 7:46** (KJV) *"Who found favour before God, and desired to find a tabernacle for the God of Jacob."*

50. **2 Corinthians 8:9** (KJV) *"For you know the grace of our Lord Jesus Christ that, though He was rich, yet for your sakes He became poor, that ye through His poverty might be rich."*

51. **2 Corinthians 9:8** (KJV) *"And God is able to make all grace to abound toward you; that ye, always having all sufficiency in all things, may abound to every good work."*

EPILOGUE

I want to thank you for taking time to read this book. God's Word is His seed and it produces after its kind. I am believing God with you that His supernatural favour will manifest in your life in a greater way than ever before.

Prayerfully reading this book again will help you get a more solid foundation for divine favour. God loves you and has great plans for your life. Remember God's Word will not return to Him void, It will prosper in that which He sends It to do. **Isaiah 55:11-12.**

You can contact me for more Christian ministry on: elnainChrist@yahoo.co.uk or +263 773290258.

You are blessed.
Apostle Ephiel Mukamuri
(Please take special note that this book is published after the author has already gone Home to be with the Lord Jesus Christ)

Printed in the United States
By Bookmasters